DRACULA

adapted from Bram Stoker's novel by

Liz Lochhead

NICK HERN BOOKS

London

www.nickhernbooks.co.uk

A Nick Hern Book

This revised version of *Dracula* first published in 2009 by Nick Hern Books Limited, 14 Larden Road, London W3 7ST

Reprinted 2010

First published in an earlier version in 1989 by Penguin Books, London

Dracula copyright © 1988, 2009 Liz Lochhead
Introduction copyright © 2009 Liz Lochhead

Liz Lochhead has asserted her right to be identified as the author of this work

Cover images: © iStockphoto.com
Cover design: Ned Hoste, 2H

Typeset by Nick Hern Books, London
Printed in the UK by CPI Antony Rowe, Chippenham, Wiltshire

A CIP catalogue record for this book is available from the British Library

ISBN 978 1 84842 029 8

FSC
Mixed Sources
Product group from well-managed forests and other controlled sources
Cert no. SGS-COC-002953
www.fsc.org
© 1996 Forest Stewardship Council

Introduction

Horace Walpole, lover of all things 'Gothick', inventing the whole genre of the Gothic novel in the eighteenth century, wrote: 'I waked one morning... from a dream of which all I could recover was that I had thought myself in an ancient castle... and that on the uppermost bannister of a great staircase I saw a gigantic hand in armour. In the evening I sat down to write.'

Mary Shelley, in her famous preface to the second edition of her *Frankenstein*, describes the early nineteenth-century genesis of her one and only – but truly great – hit: 'I did not sleep, nor could I be said to think. My imagination, unbidden, possessed and guided me... I saw the pale student of unhallowed arts kneeling beside the thing he had put together... He sleeps; but he is awakened... behold the horrid thing stands at his bedside... looking on him with yellow, watery but speculative eyes. I opened mine in terror.' A waking nightmare then? (And her own description perhaps the very source of the age-old confusion between the creator and the created? It's Frankenstein, not the Creature, that is the locus of the initial horror.) Oh, the intense excitement of the idea which, with those eyes wide open, broke in upon her: 'I have found it! What terrified me will terrify others... I need only describe the spectre which had haunted my midnight pillow.' Inspired, she sat down and began to write.

At the end of the nineteenth century Bram Stoker sat him down and he began to write something that similarly burst its novelistic bonds to become a lasting, pure and popular *myth*. Dracula truly is the immortal undead, stake him through the heart as we do again and again in comic books and the late-night films that broadcast terror through the airways and enter our dreams. (It's been said that Dracula has no shadow, because he *is* the shadow.) And Bram Stoker, his biographers report, also claimed to owe the genesis of the only work for which *he* is remembered, to a powerful nightmare.

My adaptation – a very free one it seems to me now, though a very faithful one it felt to me at the time – wasn't called up in me by a dream. It was a case of first the phone call.

It is almost twenty-five years ago, almost half a lifetime, since Ian Wooldridge, then the newish Artistic Director of the Royal Lyceum Theatre in Edinburgh, called me – I think it was already the beginning of September — to ask if I'd like to do an adaptation of Dracula, scheduled in the programme for the following spring. Looking back, I suppose either someone else had let him down at that late date, or the rights weren't available for an adaptation he wanted to use. I have no reason to imagine I would have been his first choice for the job.

I really didn't think it sounded like my cup of tea either. 'Probably just because he knows I wrote *Blood and Ice* (my first and, back then, only full-length play) about the Shelleys, Byron and the creation of *Frankenstein*, Ian imagines that I have a taste for the horror genre – and I *don't*,' I thought.

I was ashamed, though not as much as I ought to have been, to admit I'd never actually read the Bram Stoker classic. (My prejudice was that it was going to be very *fin de siècle* and sick — and probably *very badly written*.) But I said that I would do so and get back to him within the week. Next morning first thing I phoned and said I'd do it. No one else was getting this job!

This was after a sleepless night when I couldn't put the book down, my hair standing on end at what was certainly very *fin de siècle* and very sick, but very compelling, what with mad Renfield in his lunatic asylum eating flies and playing John the Baptist to his coming master, muttering his not-so-cryptic prophesies; and with Lucy's description of her 'dream' of flying with the red-eyed one above the lighthouse at Whitby; and Jonathan's 'dream' (identical to Stoker's own initiating one, apparently) of the three Vampire Brides' advances upon him ('There are kisses for us all…') and of their being repelled at the last minute by the furious Dracula ('This man belongs to me!').

My 'Yes!' phone call was before I'd even got to the abducted children; or 'the loving hand' of Lucy's fiancé staking her through the heart in her coffin 'to bring her peace'; or that shocking rape-like bit where, with Mina's newly-wed husband Jonathan asleep in a flushed stupor by her side, Dracula, at her throat, takes his fill of her life's-blood before ripping open a vein in his own breast and 'like a child forcing a kitten's nose into a saucer of milk to compel it to drink' makes her suck at and swallow his.

Well, talk about 'polymorphously perverse' – you don't have to be a psychoanalyst to have a field day with Bram Stoker's sole masterpiece. Such scenes...

Still, what really attracted me, above all, to the story, what compelled me to say yes, gave me my 'in' to the whole thing, was Rule One for becoming a vampire-victim: 'First of all you have to invite him in.'

What unappeased hunger in Lucy would cause her to invite him in?

As the eminently sensible, and psychically supremely healthy, maid Florrie – she's my own invention, she doesn't exist in Stoker's novel – says when the already infected, already addicted, already dying Lucy is terrified by a scratching, a flapping at the window: 'I didn't say bogies didn't exist, I just say bogies is all kinds and sorts of things except bogies.'

'Vampires exist. Vampires exist where men believe them to,' says the sceptical, rational psychiatrist, Seward, before Van Helsing, along with the terrible happenings described so vividly in Stoker's 'workaday prose' from so many different corroborating, matter-of-fact reports, letters and sources (all of which make for the verisimilitude of this epistolary novel), finally convince him there really are more things in heaven and earth than are dreamed of in his psychology.

'First of all you had to invite him in...' Wonderful. I sat down and I began to write.

There were Lucy and Mina, instantly refigured as sisters, in their garden by the sea; there, next door to that weird house, Carfax, which Jonathan Harker was surveying to sell to his overseas buyer, was the madhouse in London, where poor zoophagous Renfield raved...

Rereading it now, my version – and I haven't for years – I see what a strong debt the whole atmosphere of it owes to my other reading at the time. My appetites have always found deeply satisfying the work of Isak Dinesen (real name: Karen Blixen, the Danish baroness, author of *Out of Africa*), whose *Seven Gothic Tales* and, especially, her *Winter's Tales* are so pervaded by loneliness and longing. And an aching luminous loveliness and 'bottomless wisdom'. She's like an even more deeply visionary and romantic Hans Christian Andersen – for grown-ups, though.

I also by then had read, and reread – it's so gorgeous — *The Bloody Chamber,* by the great and original Angela Carter, whose equally delicious but deliberately more ornate and baroquely romantic tales were also soul food for the feminine imagination.

'*The Bloody Chamber* is like a multifaceted glittering diamond reflecting and refracting a variety of portraits of desire and sexuality – heterosexual female sexuality – which, unusually for the time, 1979, are told from a heterosexual female viewpoint,' writes Helen Simpson in her introduction to a brand new edition of the book a couple of years ago.

I always knew – who couldn't? – that *Dracula* was a narrative of suppressed sexuality and sexual guilt, but I am amazed at how much this, and especially *heterosexual female* sexual guilt, which I felt – oh, quite erroneously obviously – that I was both above and beyond by 1985, pervades my own account of the tale on subterranean levels.

I haven't reread Bram Stoker's *Dracula* for over twenty years now, and I am not sure I could. I think I sated myself on it then. Like Angela Carter, with her Charles Perrault and with her traditional folk and fairy tales, I suppose I was using what was latent in *Dracula* – and not *that* latent, for crying out loud! – and both making it overt and starting over with it. But, at the same time, every invention or intervention of my own was only an attempt, in a different medium, to faithfully tell that story of his.

Certainly it's a strange thing, revisiting one's own back pages. Angela Carter 'always knew she was drawn to Gothic tales, cruel tales, tales of wonder, tales of terror, fabulous narratives that deal directly with the imagery of the unconscious'. From rereading now my version of *Dracula* I seem, at that time of writing, to be in the act of becoming boldly, quite unselfconsciously and on the public stage, conscious of just how interested in the unconscious I was! If there is a strong element of pastiche, there is nothing of the spoof or the reductive in this retelling. I took it seriously. High-hokum as we all know it is, *Dracula* is truly great high-hokum.

I wasn't, in my personal life, very happy at the time, but what above all I remember is the deep comfort I found that winter in the intensity, almost Gothic intensity, of all that obsessive writing and rewriting.

As they say, the consolation of imaginary things is not imaginary consolation.

Liz Lochhead
May 2009

Thanks

The author would like to thank Ian Wooldridge for commissioning *Dracula*, Hugh Hodgart for nursing it through several drafts and the entire first cast at the Royal Lyceum Theatre, Edinburgh, for the many excellent contributions they made to the script.

Dracula, in a slightly different version, was first performed at the Royal Lyceum Theatre, Edinburgh, on 13 March 1985, with the following cast:

MINA WESTERMAN	Patricia Ross
LUCY WESTERMAN	Irene McDougall
FLORRIE HATHERSAGE	Tamara Kennedy
MRS MANNERS /	
DOCTOR GOLDMAN /	
NURSE NISBETT /	
NURSE GRICE	Vari Sylvester
ARTHUR SEWARD	Laurie Ventrie
JONATHAN HARKER	Robin Sneller
DRACULA	John McGlynn
VAN HELSING	Sean McCarthy
RENFIELD	Tam Dean Burn

Other parts played by members of the company.

Director	Hugh Hodgart
Designer	Gregory Smith
Composer	David McNiven

DRACULA

Liz Lochhead

from the novel by Bram Stoker

Characters

MINA WESTERMAN

LUCY WESTERMAN / VAMPIRE BRIDE 3

FLORRIE HATHERSAGE / VAMPIRE BRIDE 2

MRS MANNERS / DOCTOR GOLDMAN / NURSE NISBETT
/ NURSE GRICE / VAMPIRE BRIDE 1

DOCTOR ARTHUR SEWARD

JONATHAN HARKER

COUNT VLAD DRACULA

VAN HELSING

MALE ORDERLY DRINKWATER

NURSES / MAIDS

ACT ONE

Scene One

Heartwood House, White Bay, Whitby. The garden. Midsummer morning – a beauty, clear, clean and smelling of the sea. The garden is all dappled leafy light and there's a swing on which LUCY WESTERMAN, *out in her underwear, is swinging – with her armful of frou-frou petticoats, mirror in hand, singing her song and dreaming her young-girl dreams.*

LUCY (*singing*).
> Who shall I marry
> Tom, Dick or Harry?

She kisses her own lovely reflection in the mirror.

Enter MINA WESTERMAN, *her big sister, proper English rose, a peach, eating one.*

MINA. Catch her death! Lucy, what can you be thinking of?

LUCY. Come lace me up, sis. There's a love.

MINA. Do hurry up, my angel, he'll be here soon...

LUCY. Tighter. Tighter, Mina...

MINA. I'll hurt you.

LUCY. No, you won't. I want it tighter. I want to feel it nip me in. The day they put me in stays and made me wear my hair up I swore blind if I was to be pinched and skewered then I was to have the thinnest, thinnest waist and the highest, highest hair. I wasn't going to suffer for nothing and not be noticed. Oh, Mina, aren't you pretty in your silk? You look good enough to eat.

MINA. Hold still, oh... Lucy, he'll be here soon!

LUCY. And me not done dolling myself... Maybe I'll get him to come and catch me.

MINA (*distracted*). Mmm, pet?

LUCY. I said, meine Wilhel-Mina, maybe I'll take my time and laze and dawdle and let my curling tongs go quite cold and let him come and gawp at me in my drawers.

MINA. Lucy!

LUCY. Wouldn't that give him a fright? And a sight to remember. What you going to give him before he goes away?

MINA. Lucy! I don't know what you mean.

LUCY. Well, he is your fiancé, for goodness' sake! You are practically married.

MINA. We are *not* 'practically married'. It's weeks and weeks yet till my birthday. He'll go away. And then he'll come back. And *then* we'll be married.

LUCY. And him going off on such a long journey. What are you going to give him to remember you by?

MINA. My likeness. In a locket.

LUCY. And he'll keep you in his pocket. Take you out to look at… Nothing else?

MINA. Nothing. Else my mother would turn in her grave! I'm supposed to set you an example. You! What about the example naughty little sisters set sensible big sisters?

LUCY. It's only tease… only talk.

MINA. Well, you watch your mouth, miss!

By now they're as buttoned up as each other. MINA *begins to fix* LUCY's *hair.* LUCY *sighs.*

LUCY. Sometimes I can't help think…

MINA. What?

LUCY. Nothing… (*A sigh.*) Just…

MINA. Just what?

LUCY. Just, I wish something was going to happen to me.

MINA. It will. One day.

LUCY. It would be so lovely to go on a honeymoon. Oh, Mina, you're so lucky. I wish I was waiting for my wedding dress to come from Paris. I wish I had a Jonathan.

MINA. Hands off, miss! He's mine.

LUCY. He's Mina's. Mustn't forget. Tied and true. And... due here any time!

She begins scurrying about, tidying up and dropping things again.

Behold, the bridegroom cometh! Into the life of lovely Wilhelmina Westerman the twenty-four-year-old heiress and sister to the lynx-eyed Lucy – Enter: Ta-ra! Jonathan Harker, tall, dark, handsome, blue-eyed, articled clerk extraordinaire –

MINA (*laughing*). Listen, miss, he got his exams. He passed. He's a solicitor. And *you* read too many penny dreadfuls!

LUCY. And you know how I like my penny dreadfuls.

MINA. How's that?

LUCY. Two-pence-coloured!

The girls run off laughing.

Scene Two

Bedlam. Suddenly it's all grim NURSES *with fouled laundry in the asylum.*

RENFIELD *and* DOCTOR ARTHUR SEWARD *together. In and out of sight, sometimes, elsewhere from them,* DOCTOR GOLDMAN, *a lady psychiatrist with notebook, writing.* RENFIELD *is shaved by a* NURSE *or* ORDERLY. *Rocking back and forth, he sometimes catcalls and chants. He is presently gabbling maniacally.*

RENFIELD. I once knew a woman who swallowed a fly. Perhaps she'll die. Perhaps she won't die. To die or not to die,

that is the question. BED-LAM BED-LAM BED-LAM BED-LAM. Bats in the belfry, bats, set of screw-looses… screw Lucy's screw Lucy's screw Lucy's. It's cold. Getting colder. Time to get yourself into something warm and double-breasted in a whorehouse, my son. I once knew a woman. Who swallowed a… spider that wriggled and tickled and tickled inside her… Doctor Seward! Sewer. Lord Muck-mind. Mr Pissriver. Shit floats! Doctor Seward, you bastard.

SEWARD. Come, Mr Renfield, calm yourself, man. Swallow this opiate, sir, it'll make you more lucid.

RENFIELD. Lucid. Lucy'd. Lucy'd. She would. She-swallowed-the-cat-to-catch-the-bird-she-swallowed-the-swallow-to-catch-the-spider-she-swallowed-the-spider-to-catch-the-fly-but-I-don't-know-why… (*Pause.*) Doctor Seward? Doctor Seward, I feel empty.

SEWARD. You'll feel better, Mr Renfield.

NURSE *administers dose.* GOLDMAN *is in mid-spiel of her deliberations.*

GOLDMAN. …One might hypothesise, Silberman says, that the *animus* in its negative, demonic phase lures women away from all human relationships and especially from all contacts with real men…

RENFIELD (*melancholic, pitiful*). Empty. They took me and they de-loused me. They shaved me and they salted me with lye. (*Angry.*) They wormed me like a dog and they wired me up to their bad machines.

SEWARD (*amused*). Really, Mr Renfield? And what sort of… bad machines?

RENFIELD. They shoved rubber in my gob to stop it, gave me something bitter and sweet to bite on, and they fastened wires to my temples. My whole head is a temple. Full of precious things for my master to come and worship. Because he's coming in his warship. My-master-that-I-worship-is-coming-in-his-warship. (*Pause.*) The machine took the current of my memories away. My memories that fed me… and fed from me… and bled me like leeches and drained my life away. Now I'm empty. I feed on no life and no life feeds from me.

Buzz of a fly. Louder and louder and RENFIELD'*s mad eyes watching it.*

GOLDMAN (*in mid-spiel again*). ...correspondingly the malign or 'shadow' *anima* in a man involves him in those neurotic pseudo-intellectual dialogues that inhibit him from getting into direct touch with life so that, starved of spontaneity and outgoing feeling, he cannot live it...

She passes SEWARD, *muttering and writing. Exits.*

SEWARD (*muttering*). ...Lord, I do sympathise with those who deem it difficult to distinguish the physicians from the afflicted in this institution... Doctor Goldman! Christ, what a crab apple.

SEWARD *begins to watch* RENFIELD *watching the fly. Suddenly* RENFIELD *snatches it from the air. Buzz stops. He opens his hand a bit. Buzz again. He picks it up, still fizzing between thumb and forefinger and eats it with a sickening crunch.* SEWARD *shudders.*

RENFIELD (*defiant*). It's fat with life, strong life, and gives life to me. Very good, very tasty, very wholesome. I know a doctor who should try some.

SEWARD (*amused*). Ingested insects?

RENFIELD. Some life.

SEWARD. In Mr Renfield's case I recommend that his medication be continued, increasing by one milligram per day over the next two weeks in my absence, until exactly twice his present dose... Diet. Minimum. Cereals. Pulses. No stimulants.

He has been looking out of the window during some of the last.

Good God! Jonathan Harker. I do believe... yes, it is Jonathan Harker. What the hell is he doing wandering around in all that undergrowth? Orderly! Orderly!

ORDERLY DRINKWATER *comes.*

Mr Drinkwater! Will you please go down for me into the grounds and fetch that man taking all the photographs of

Carfax and tell him Doctor Seward – No! Say Seward Major requires the presence of Harker Minimus in his study forthwith.

DRINKWATER *stares*.

Go on, man, he'll know exactly what I mean.

DRINKWATER *goes*.

RENFIELD. Help me, Doctor Seward, help me! Listen, listen, they put things in my food, they do!

SEWARD. Young Jonty Harker, well, well…

He is looking out of the window for DRINKWATER *to approach* JONATHAN, *and isn't listening to* RENFIELD's *babbling fear*.

RENFIELD. The Beldams of Bedlam sans merci, Doctor, they are poisoning me.

SEWARD. Carfax! Why the devil anyone would want to photograph an architectural monstrosity like that is utterly beyond me…

SEWARD *exits, paying no attention to his increasingly desperate patient*.

RENFIELD. They put things in. Bad stuff. Puss, piss, jiss, bad blood and mother's milk, it open up my head to him, you got to listen, help me or he get in. The poison make me want to let him in. He say, let me, I come in your head to throb in your temples with the golden altars and the swelling organs and the ruby ruby light from the high windows will spill, spill on the floor my power and my glory. I say no I say no I shut my mouth ears nose eyes I say no he say yes he say isn't it shame isn't disgrace I'll get in though it be not through the hole in your face. Doctor! You leave me alone and scared and I want to let him in. Help me, Doctor Seward, I don't want to want to let him in…

RENFIELD *falls to the ground*.

Scene Three

SEWARD*'s private study/sitting room.* SEWARD *with*
JONATHAN HARKER. *Brandy in balloons and cigars.*

SEWARD. And I just couldn't believe it. Seeing an old Norwellian in this neck of the woods!

JONATHAN. Imagine my surprise! The face of Norwell's
strictest prefect –

SEWARD. Strict but fair!

JONATHAN. A monster! The voice that could send a thousand
little boys scurrying to butter his crumpets, sugar his tea, find
another pot of cherry conserve!

SEWARD. How many terms was it you fagged for me,
Jonathan? Was it two or was it three? I must have been a
perfect beast.

JONATHAN. Actually, looking back on our sainted schooldays, I
suppose the last face I ought to be surprised to see hanging
out of the bars of a madhouse window is that of an old
Norwellian.

SEWARD. Happy days, eh?

JONATHAN. I'll drink to them being over.

SEWARD. And now little Harker Minimus is engaged to be
married? Ah-ah, I read the announcement in *The Times*. Miss
Westerman, eh? The sugar millionairess! Well, well, I thought
to myself, that's marrying *trade*, but I suppose these days
being the youngest son of a baronet doesn't pay many bar bills.

JONATHAN. You scholarship boys always were the worst
snobs! Mina is the loveliest girl who ever lived and I should
marry her if she hadn't two brass farthings to rub together.

SEWARD. Hark at Harker! Jonty, my dear friend, I am only
teasing you. I am sure Miss Westerman is charming in every
way, or you'd not love her.

JONATHAN. She is beautiful. And brave. And clever.

SEWARD. And sweet?

JONATHAN. And sweet. You've not married then, Arthur? Been avoiding matrimony like the pit of hell?

SEWARD. I've not married. Yet. Ah, Jonathan, when I was twenty and hard at my studies I thought I'll marry at twenty-five; at twenty-five I thought thirty was a fine age for a man to settle down; and now I'm thirty…

JONATHAN. Don't leave it too long, Art.

SEWARD. I won't leave it too long. What woman though would marry into a madhouse?

JONATHAN. Plenty do.

SEWARD. Yes, but my wife would have to do it knowingly.

Pause.

JONATHAN. I'm sure you work too hard. You should… take a holiday. You said you have some annual leave –

SEWARD. Holidays. Honestly, Jonathan, holidays… bore me. I don't know what to do with myself for the first couple of days. I read, I toss, I turn. Mostly I'm glad to be back with my charges and sure I'm doing something useful again.

JONATHAN. Come with me.

SEWARD. What?

JONATHAN. I mean it. You'll enjoy it. Tonight I catch the overnight from King's Cross for Whitby. I am going to spend two or three days with Mina before I go off on that long business trip.

SEWARD. To see your foreign nobleman… And, do I get you right, you've actually managed to flog him Carfax?

JONATHAN. A very desirable property. Ask the estate agent. He'll tell you so himself! 'Castellated dwelling-house, late medieval but with numerous additions from later centuries. Notably a fine Tudor *gingerbread* chimney with priest hole. Restoration west wing. Banqueting hall with *trompe-l'œil* ceiling, Wren cupola, Regency drawing room featuring fine Adam fireplace, et cetera, et cetera.'

SEWARD. Yes, well… all a bit Gothic for my tastes.

JONATHAN. Oh, but he loves it.

SEWARD. Does he know his soon-to-be next-door neighbours here are somewhat – ?

JONATHAN. Batty? (*Laughs.*) Well, Mr Hawkins and the estate agent we did the deal with did not seem to think it was strictly… relevant.

SEWARD. Poor man, he doesn't know what's in store for him. On the nights of the full moon when all the lunatics –

JONATHAN. Go loopy? Do they? Does the moon actually –

SEWARD. Not at all, Jonathan. Sheer superstition and stories. No, I am afraid that all the clinical, if not the neurotic, mental illnesses are all simply a matter of imbalances in the complex chemicals of one cortex of the brain. Your… Count Dracula will find we have our inmates tame and docile and not at all antisocial as neighbours.

JONATHAN. But you will come? To Whitby?

SEWARD. No, Jonathan. I think not.

JONATHAN. Yes, Arthur, come. Come on one condition. That you make quite quite sure you don't let my Mina make a busman's holiday of it for you. You see, she has this little sister. Lucy. Sweet kid really. Mina, though… Mina worries terribly about her. Well, last year after their father died, Lucy went into a sort of decline… got terribly terribly thin and somewhat… feverish in her behaviour.

SEWARD. Did she have a loss of normal female functions?

JONATHAN. How on earth would I know?

SEWARD. Forgive me. I'm a doctor. I forget how to address laymen… Probably simple girlish hysteria. Attention-seeking behaviour. Whatever the Silbermans and Goldmans say! Nine times out of ten, rest, companionship, some exercise mental and physical – and wait for little miss to grow out of it.

JONATHAN. But you'll come?

SEWARD. I'll come. Why not – if we can travel first class. Let's go and organise the tickets!

JONATHAN. Now, if I'd done as I intended and gone back to the office, my Miss Bell could have arranged it all for us.

SEWARD. Miss Bell?

JONATHAN. My secretary.

SEWARD. Stenographer, eh? And what's she like to work late at the office with?

JONATHAN. Miss Bell? A peach. A poppet. Actually, yes, she is quite quite delicious…

SEWARD. And you are a married man.

JONATHAN. Practically. Yield not to temptation…

SEWARD. Well, I'm sure I'm in the wrong job. What have I got but dog-faced Austrian blue-stocking doctors and boot-faced nurses with bad breath? Tickets!

JONATHAN (*as they exit*). But, Arthur, if all I've heard about nurses, is true, then…

Scene Four

Bedlam. RENFIELD *with* DRINKWATER, *and* NURSE GRICE, *a sadist.* RENFIELD *is chained up, sniffling and snuffing like a dog.*

GRICE. 'Mon now, Mr Renfield, drink up your nice medicine or Doctor Seward won't come back and take you walkies. Won't bring you back no nice rock from seaside. Give it him, Mr Drinkwater.

RENFIELD *sniffs and points like a setter.* DRINKWATER *spoons stuff into him as he fawns and licks servilely.*

Good doggie, scoff up your Bob Martin's.

RENFIELD *takes mouthfuls of it then, as* DRINKWATER *stands back, spits a mouthful right in* GRICE's *face.*

You stupid stupid cur! Kick him. Kick him from dawn to dusk and back again!

As DRINKWATER *goes to kick him,* RENFIELD *quickly sits up and begs, tongue out, his eyes warning.* DRINKWATER *hesitates.*

Kick the shit out of him!

DRINKWATER *can't, he stands back.* RENFIELD *stands up, lucid, graceful, and picks up birds in cages. Holds them out and, standing with them like scales of justice, raising and lowering, he speaks first to* DRINKWATER, *then to* GRICE.

RENFIELD. My master will bless you. He'll punish you! My master is at hand. And I am here to obey his every command. See the moon, Mr Drinkwater, how sweetly she sail, she wax once, she wane, and my master, my master he come again. Oh yes, Nurse Grice, him come! And me? Me, I sit, I sit with my birds in the wilderness, pretty birds, little victims, pretty ones, how they do flutter! The *struggling* sacrifice, Nurse Grice, ain't it nice, *that* do quicken the heart, *that* give a little flutter…

GRICE. Mad bastard! No wonder I'd not come in to you alone. Drinkwater, I'm putting you down on report. Disobeying orders. And him! Fuckin' fevvers in his teeth. Eatin' sparrers.

Exit GRICE *and* DRINKWATER.

RENFIELD. Prophet in the wilderness, proclaiming his coming: 'Full moon when next she sail, I sail with her, I come.'

Scene Five

Heartwood House. The garden again. As the table is set, and JONATHAN *is fiddling around with his camera,* MINA *is tippy-typing away in the garden to one side and* MRS MANNERS *goes out and in, supervising the table and the serving* MAIDS.

MINA. All right! Positively the last letter before lunch. And only if you promise to help me finalise this guestlist after.

JONATHAN. Watch the birdie!

MINA. And don't I cut a pretty picture? I'm sure I'm just as fast a typist as your Miss Thing.

JONATHAN. Bell.

MINA. What's she like anyway?

JONATHAN. Who?

MINA. Miss Bell.

JONATHAN. A dragon. Absolutely.

He dives under the camera hood.

MINA. All right, fire away.

JONATHAN. What?

MINA. Your letter.

JONATHAN. Okay.

He goes round behind MINA *and kisses her, cupping his hands around her breasts.* MRS MANNERS *enters.*

Are you in a position to take a little dictation?

MINA. I'm all ears. And fingertips.

She sees MRS MANNERS*, extricates herself.*

JONATHAN. Very well. Take a letter, Miss Westerman! Messrs Hardcastle, Hawkins, Hawkins and Harker, solicitors at law, number seven, The Crescent, et cetera... To: Count Vlad Dracula –

Gong strikes to announce lunch. Enter LUCY*, dragging a slightly flushed and energised* SEWARD*.* JONATHAN *photographs* LUCY *and* SEWARD *together, posing, smiling. They kiss, unseen by* MINA*.* JONATHAN*, smiling too, goes to join them at the lunch table.*

FLORRIE*, the new maid, is very young, very pretty and just a little nervous. She is silver-servicing some chicken in a cold sauce. Goes to* MINA*.*

MINA. Gentlemen first, Florrie! Guests.

FLORRIE. Sorry, miss...

FLORRIE *goes to* SEWARD.

SEWARD. Yes. Thank you. Yes. That's enough.

FLORRIE. Leg or breast, Mr Jonathan?

JONATHAN. Pardon?

FLORRIE. The chicken, sir. Leg or breast?

JONATHAN. Breast. No. Leg. Leg. Breast… I think… emm… could I have a little piece of each please, Florrie?

FLORRIE. Certainly, Mr Jonathan, sir.

MINA. Just a little! No, that's too much. Fine, thank you, Florrie.

LUCY. No thanks, no, I'm not in the least bit hungry.

SEWARD. Lucy, you ought to have a little…

MINA. Try some, Lucy. For me, please!

LUCY. No, thank you!

FLORRIE. A bit more, Mr Jonathan?

LUCY. Saucy!

MINA. That's quite everything for now, thank you, Florrie!

JONATHAN. This sauce smells absolutely delicious.

FLORRIE *exits*. MRS MANNERS *gives the table an imperious head-waitery once-over and exits too*.

MINA. And so, Arthur, you are not wearied of our company yet? We are flattered we can amuse you.

SEWARD. Indeed, Mina, I have spent three of the happiest days of my life here with you… and Lucy. The air is like… champagne.

LUCY. Very salty champagne!

MINA. I am sorry I have had to be so possessive with Jonathan, Arthur. Business to do with the wedding. Decisions to be made.

JONATHAN. I hate making decisions.

MINA. Don't I know it! Honestly, Arthur, you'd think that the most brilliant young solicitor of his generation would be able to choose between red roses and white for the floral arrangements.

LUCY. Arthur…

She nudges him and whispers. He puts a finger to his lips.

JONATHAN. I can't see it matters. As long as you marry me, Mina. Soon.

MINA. It's soon all right – and the fabric for our dresses not arrived yet!

JONATHAN. You've not been finding it difficult to amuse your-self, Arthur?

SEWARD. Indeed not! Lucy and I have been walking… and riding. And yesterday even sea-bathing.

LUCY. I did not go in.

SEWARD. But you watched me.

LUCY. Arthur swam so far out, Mina, he got smaller and smaller and smaller till his head was just a little dot in all the heaving grey ocean. I got frightened and I called him. I screamed.

SEWARD. Dear Lucy, I was all right, everything was under control, I'm a very strong swimmer, everything was… quite all right.

MINA. My sister gets very nervous about things, Arthur…

LUCY. Oh yes, crazy Lucy, mad sleepwalking skinny Lucy with her migraines and her over-vivid imagination. I know what you say about me behind my back, you bitch, Mina, I wish you weren't my bloody sister!

She rushes out in floods of tears.

JONATHAN (*standing up*). Lucy, my pet, sit down, don't –

MINA. Leave her, Jonathan, she's only after attention.

JONATHAN. Then shouldn't she get some?

MINA. Sheer tantrum!

JONATHAN. Arthur? Can't you…?

SEWARD. I am afraid I cannot take Lucy as any kind of patient or give you any advice of a medical nature concerning her. For personal reasons. For *ethical* reasons. You see, today I asked Lucy Westerman if she would consent to be my wife. And she said yes.

JONATHAN. Arthur, you old devil… I had no idea. Mina! Isn't this the most –

MINA. My sister, Doctor Seward, is eighteen years old. A child! Someone of your age must see she is far too young and unstable to enter into such an arrangement.

JONATHAN. Mina!

SEWARD. Miss Westerman, I am sorry to have… sprung this news on you so precipitously. It must be something of a shock. I hope you will learn to approve of me in time and see that your sister's health and future happiness is my every desire and concern. Now, if you'll excuse me, with your permission I'll go to your sister and see if she'll walk with me in the garden, well wrapped-up of course. I'll see if I can be of some comfort to my fiancée.

SEWARD *exits*.

JONATHAN. Oh, Mina, Mina!

MINA *bursts into tears*. JONATHAN *moves over to her side in an instant, takes her in his arms and comforts her and kisses her.*

MINA. Oh, Jonathan, I am so sorry. What must your friend think of me? Hold me…

JONATHAN. It's all this wedding business! Lists! Flowers! Who cares! Mina, come with me, come with me tomorrow, marry me in London, come with me and we'll make a mad honeymoon of my business trip. You can be my secretary.

MINA. Jonathan! My inheritance.

JONATHAN. Don't let's wait for it. I don't care about the money. We don't need the money. I can make my living as a solicitor. Marry me tomorrow.

MINA. You must be mad, Jonathan! I'm… just being silly, I'm sorry, sweetheart, it's… all this… wedding business… Oh, Jonathan, please, please don't go to Europe tomorrow. Don't go away.

JONATHAN. Mina, Mina, Mina, whatever is the matter?

MINA. Such dreams, Jonathan, such horrible horrible dreams…
and premonitions… Oh! I know it's silly…

JONATHAN. Mina, let me come and sleep with you tonight.

MINA. Jonathan!

JONATHAN. Let me come. I'll hug you close and keep all the
bogeymen away.

MINA. Oh, Jonathan, we cannot – not here at Heartwood, Mrs
Manners would know – and Florrie and Lucy and… everyone.

JONATHAN. Mina, I'll sneak into your room secretly after
everyone is asleep. Damn it, who cares if they know? I love
you. Let me love you.

MINA. We must wait for our wedding.

JONATHAN. Mina –

MINA. No, Jonathan, I mean it. Absolutely no.

(*A blurt*.) You can come and stay with me tonight if you
promise not to go away tomorrow.

JONATHAN. I can't do that, Mina. Mr Hawkins, the senior
partner, has trusted me with all this vital business with the
Count. It's my career, Mina.

MINA. God forbid you should jeopardise your precious career
on my account.

JONATHAN. Mina!

MINA. And now I'm going to see my sister… and her…
fiancé… and make apologies to them for my behaviour. I pray
she may be happier in her betrothal than I am in mine. Don't
dare come after me! Go away!

MINA *exits*.

Scene Six

Bedlam. NURSE NISBETT *comes with a bowl of gristly brown stew, for* RENFIELD; *she is a masochist, played by the same actress as* GRICE.

RENFIELD. Go away!

NISBETT. Mr Renfield, Mr Renfield, it's me, Nisbett, wiv sommat for you. Don't you fancy a little somethin'?

RENFIELD. Not hungry!

NISBETT. Take a bit, do then. Must be famished. Bastard clever-dick doctor putting you on starvation rations. He doesn't care! 'Doctor Seward, sir, Mr Renfield ett another sparrer. He did, sir. Coughed it up not half-hour after in a pool of puke and blood and feathers.' I wouldn't treat a dog like he treats you, Mr Renfield, I call it a sin. Experimenting. Doctor bloody God Almighty, eh? Seeing how far you'll go. Well, stands to reason, there be just no knowing how far a man'll go, you give him nothin'! Sick as a dog, poor lamb.

RENFIELD *puts his hands over his ears, rocking and singing in loud monotone right in her face.*

RENFIELD (*singing*).
Who ate Cock Robin,
My head is throbbin',
The sweet sound of sobbin', sobbin', sobbin'…

NISBETT. Yes. I wouldn't care, only it's me got to clean it up!

(*Pause.*) Now then, it's not a lot and it's not hot but what I got I'll give it all to you, poor Mr Renfield.

He dashes the plate and spoon out of her hands, and all over her apron goes the brown stew. She screams.

Scalded! Scalded me! You madman, that's the last time I ever try to help you…

She runs off, sobbing. Lights up slowly, very slowly on DRACULA's *castle.*

RENFIELD.
> Come into my parlour,
> Said the spider
> To the fly.

Perhaps you'll die. Would you care to dine with me? Would you care to die with me...

> Something inanimate,
> Something on a plate,
> Is something I hate.

See, I think it's not nice, eating dead things, not nice to take a bit out of something that can't bite back. I call that... necrophiliac.

Not a very savoury appetite. Not polite. Now something blood heat... that's what I call sweet. If it moves, eat it.

He cracks one between his teeth with pleasure.

> Yes, come
> Into my parlour,
> Said the spider
> To the fly.

Scene Seven

DRACULA's *castle. Doors swing open and* JONATHAN *enters. No one there.*

JONATHAN (*tentatively*). Count Dracula...?

Nothing. No one.

Suddenly DRACULA *himself is there.*

DRACULA. At last. I am Dracula. Welcome. Enter of your own will. Come freely. Go freely. And leave something of the happiness you bring.

JONATHAN. Jonathan Harker. (*Hand outstretched.*) Count Dracula?

Let me tell you, I am pleased to see you, sir! My journey has been a nightmare...

DRACULA. Come. Well come. Liberty Hall to you, dear friend. Remember. What's mine is yours.

JONATHAN (*almost laughing in relief*). If it wasn't storms... and lightning fit to split the sky... and wind... and wolves. Wolves! You should have heard them!

DRACULA. Ah... Harker Jonathan.

JONATHAN. Sorry?

DRACULA. Apologies. I used my country's habit of putting the patronymic first. Jonathan. Mr Harker, my friend, you are evidently one of those that have ears to hear.

JONATHAN. Er...

DRACULA. But I have the manners of a barbarian. Yes? You are hungry. Evidently. So. *Paprika Hendl*. It is, among our peasantry, something of a national dish. On feast days. And the day you deliver yourself to me, that is a feast day. Yes? Certainly...

JONATHAN. You are not dining yourself?

DRACULA. Forgive me, I have supped earlier. Is good?

JONATHAN. Incredibly good! Mmm. Strange seasoning. I have been making quite a collection of recipes here I hope my Mina'll establish with cook as staples in our household. Have you ever tasted 'robber steak'? It's bits of bacon, beef, onion – a mushroom or two sometimes – and it's sort of skewered on to sticks and simply –

DRACULA. No, Mr Harker, I do not care to eat this 'robber steak'. Excuse me. My appetites have grown capricious in my old age... Not everything agrees with me. Nevertheless I know what I like. Simple things.

JONATHAN *eats – gradually reviving at the food and a glass of Old Tokay*. DRACULA *surveys* JONATHAN *when he's tucking in*.

This... my Carfax is fine castle?

JONATHAN. Castle? Well… Mm! Letter from Mr Hawkins. Forgive me!

Gives the letter to DRACULA *out of his heart pocket.*

It is – you have seen the photographs I sent? – a substantial mansion. It will make a fine home.

DRACULA. And every Englishman's home is his castle, don't you say so? Well, I shall make me a fine English man. (*Pause.*) Carfax. Is strange name, yes? Perhaps from the French. *Quatre Faces.* Such corruption of language interests me much. 'Four Sides.' Ah well, I suppose there are at least four sides to every question. Is that not so, Mr Harker?

JONATHAN. I should say so! Mina would say that is the trouble with me – I can see something to be said for them all.

DRACULA. Ah, so you cannot make up your mind, Mr Harker? Then perhaps one of your friends will have to make it up for you…

JONATHAN *looks a bit taken aback.*

Ah, my friend, forgive me. I have little society here, you may well imagine. I make you uncomfortable because I lose my lightness of touch. (*Sigh.*) So! Who is this 'Mina'? She is your wife?

JONATHAN. Practically. We will marry on her twenty-fifth birthday, in September.

DRACULA. You have a likeness of her?

JONATHAN (*fishing out photos*). Some pictures I took in the gardens of the summerhouse at Whitby they have.

DRACULA. Whitby? It is by seaside?

JONATHAN. Why, yes… it is a fishing port and rather fine resort. On the Yorkshire coast. My Kodak again!

DRACULA. Very nice.

JONATHAN. It is a remarkable house. Heartwood, it's –

DRACULA. Remarkable girls. (*Pause.*) There are three of them. Which is your… Mina? It is usual English name, this?

JONATHAN. Not very. Yes. No. It's not unusual. Especially. (*Pause*.) She's the one in the middle. That's her sister, Lucy.

DRACULA. They are not alike, these sisters?

JONATHAN. Mina and Lucy? Good Lord, no! Chalk and cheese.

DRACULA. Night and day.

She looks familiar, almost. I feel I know her. She has Slavic face, this... Lucy.

JONATHAN. Yes, I do agree. The first few days in this country I saw my sister-in-law in every other serving girl that brought me supper – it was very disconcerting, I can tell you!

DRACULA. And you have tasted the wine of the country?

JONATHAN. Sorry?

DRACULA. The Old Tokay. I am told it produce queer sting on – the tongue, but... not unpleasurable? I am sorry. We were discussing the ladies. Gentlemen's privilege, yes? And who is the third flower in this... English garden?

JONATHAN. That's Florrie – she's their maid.

DRACULA. Three pretty maids, all in a row. And you, Mr Harker, have picked the queen among princesses, yes? A proper English rose. (*Pause*.) Is very wonderful thing, this photography. Although I am sure that portrait painters do not agree with us! Each common clerk can keep his last duchess in sepia inside his pigskin wallet.

JONATHAN. I'll take your photograph! You'll love it. Of course we'll have to wait for the light – tomorrow I'll –

DRACULA. No, Mr Harker, you won't take my photograph! I am... too old and dry to say cheese and pose before your magic gadget. Believe me, it simply won't turn out. (*Pause*.) You find my country beautiful? You took many snaps?

JONATHAN. Very. Such changes of landscape... and climate even. Extraordinary!

DRACULA. Good. And my people?

JONATHAN. A fascinating mixture. They seem full of good qualities. But very very superstitious...

DRACULA. Folklore, my friend. You write it down in your recipe book. 'Fascinating mixture'? 'Mixture' is true. You are at the heart of Europe. In the deeps of the dark forest at its black heart. My country is a crossroads. No, I do not like this symbol. My country is a whirlpool. Of blood. The Berserker, the Hun, the Magyar, the Turk, he came, he conquered, he was conquered, he bred, and he bled. There have been so many battles on this soil that the earth itself... You have a phrase, I think, from your Bible? 'Flesh is grass.' I wish to turn this upside down. Here in my country the grass... is flesh.

JONATHAN. I hope we are done with wars and bloodshed. Surely as the twentieth century dawns, mankind will see sense.

DRACULA. The twentieth century! Bah, I despise this twentieth century, it disgusts me.

JONATHAN. But it hasn't even begun yet.

DRACULA. Habsburgs! Romanovs! Mongrels. Upstarts. My race, Jonathan, my house, we Székelys of the noble line of Dracule, the little dragon; we always gladly receive the bloody sword.

JONATHAN. One would think you had been present at all these battles...

DRACULA. To a Boyar, the pride of house and name is his own pride, their glory his glory, their fate his fate.

JONATHAN. I'm afraid I feel a man must make his own way in the world whatever –

DRACULA. Ah... democracy. The twentieth century. Ah yes... The warlike days are over. Blood is too precious a thing in these days of dishonourable peace. But you have come far. It is many days since you leave the Orient Express, with its smells of linen and leather and buttoned carriage-cloth... and Turkish cigarettes, if I remember well? Yes, I must move again, among men. But you can divert me. My friend can tell me his traveller's tales and take me out of myself...?

JONATHAN. I don't know that I can. So... long on the road. Trains. Traps... Diligences! Why, I even travelled a day by farmer's cart once when my train connection missed by more than five hours. His wife gave me this crucifix! (*Fishes it out*.) Pressed it on me, wouldn't take no for an answer!

DRACULA *naturally reacts to this with his classic recoil*.

DRACULA. Throw it away! Is ugly thing...

JONATHAN. I shouldn't dream of doing so. It was so kindly meant, such a good motherly face she had...

He puts it away in his pocket though, and DRACULA *recovers his aplomb*.

DRACULA. I simply meant, my friend, that it was lead. Base. I am somewhat of old snob. I cannot bear what is not old... and fine... and beautiful... and precious. That is why I live here all alone with my memories, the splendid spoils of my ancestors. (*Pause*.) If you'd throw that leaden peasant thing out of the window, I'd replace it with gold.

JONATHAN. I must keep it. It was a gift. In good faith.

DRACULA (*admitting a small defeat*). Ah, my friend, if you did not have such a warm heart you would have little to offer me indeed, believe me... Your Mr Hawkins here, he writes well of you, 'energy... talent... discreet... silent... faithful disposition which has grown with him into manhood in my service will, I am fully confident, put itself to your every use and render him malleable to your every instruction.'

JONATHAN *is somewhat disconcerted*.

So tomorrow morning you must write to our friend – and to any other who will wish word of you – and tell him you stay with me for one month from now.

JONATHAN. A month! But the business we have to do... while complicated... certainly cannot take more than a few days to complete.

DRACULA. But, my friend, I want you for... conversation.

JONATHAN. Conversation?

DRACULA. Your wonderful English language. It is a living thing, yes? I do not possess it.

JONATHAN. Count, your command is admirable.

DRACULA. Dry. Library dust on every syllable. I know the grammar and the words, but I do not know how to speak them.

JONATHAN. Your English is excellent.

DRACULA. Through my books, my friends whom I love, I have travelled all over your great country without leaving my own armchair. I am pressed by the throng of your London crowds in their brown fog. I flow with them over London Bridge, to the heart of the city. The rush of humanity, its life, its change, its death – all that makes it what it is. Books are good. But I lack the living tongue.

JONATHAN. I am no philologist –

DRACULA. I would not have you so. I want you because you are young. And ordinary. Yes. A splendid specimen of the upright young man. (*Pause*.) A good slanging! The lifeblood of the language… So, when I drink in your every word, digest it, then I shall put on my straw hat and come out from the garden of my Carfax, a real English man.

JONATHAN. Count, I cannot stay with you.

DRACULA. Ssh, no such thing as cannot. Sleep first. In the morning, believe me, you will feel differently. If there be one axiom in human affairs that be it…

A howling of wolves.

Listen. Listen to the children of the night. What music they make.

JONATHAN. Mus-ic?

DRACULA. Ah yes, music. Not a true soul but knows its melody. By heart. The first time he hear it.

JONATHAN. They curdle my blood.

DRACULA. Come, come, Mr Harker, blood is not so easily curdled. In milksop kindergartens perhaps, tales of the Big

Bad Wolf might – what do you say – scare the pretty children witless? But a man whose heart has wintered enough for him to be worth something, he hears the wolf sing to the moon his own sometime desolation and it quickens the hunter in him so in his mind he runs with that grey pack in the night. Can't you see them, flowing like a ragged wind over Russia, pouring lower than the blown grasses over the steppes? Outside, in that black forest, their eyes are more than the stars and twice as secret.

It is as if JONATHAN *is hypnotised into this next statement.*

JONATHAN. They ringed our coach – the horses screamed and plunged and stopped stock-still, and I looked out and saw them in the full moonlight. White teeth. Red tongues. Shaggy hair.

DRACULA. The dogs of nature...

JONATHAN. The other passengers were frightened. There was a girl there, she was terrified. I could feel her shiver under her thin shawl. So I held her close. For human comfort, you understand, to calm her as one would a child! She taught me words. *Ordog, Pokol, Stregioca, Vrolok, Vlkoslak*. She said... werewolf.

DRACULA *has been murmuring translations.*

DRACULA. 'Satan', 'hell', 'vampire'... Ah, my friend, girlish superstition. I am sure your reason tells you so? I can assure you: these outside you hear howling are real wolves. All animal. Were-wolves, are-wolves, and ever-more-shall-be-wolves. (*Pause.*) Ah, Jonathan, I make a joke. Is good. No? You see what life you give to my conversation already! But I overtire you.

He stands and motions JONATHAN *to his feet.*

Come. You shall make your toilet and I shall make your bed for you. No keeping of servants in this place so deep in the wood. So I, my friend, tonight I will be happy to... play the valet, or the chambermaid, whatever you will. And – you are so tired – tonight I wish you no dreams to disturb your rest.

They walk.

And so, Jonathan Harker, you have a long and a difficult journey but at last you have reached your destiny.

JONATHAN. *Destination*.

DRACULA. Ah. You see how I need you for a teacher.

Scene Eight

Heartwood House. MINA *and* FLORRIE, *in the garden*. FLORRIE *is shy*.

FLORRIE. Mrs Manners, miss, she asked me to ask you, any news, miss, o' Mr Jonathan?

MINA. No news… Florrie, you must be beginning to settle in.

FLORRIE. Yes, Miss Mina.

MINA. Are you happy here?

FLORRIE. Happy, miss?… I haven't thought to think.

MINA. I hope for you to be happy, Florrie.

FLORRIE (*curtsying*). Yes, miss.

MINA. Don't 'Yes, miss' me, that's not very familiar!

FLORRIE. No, miss.

MINA. Don't you think we can all work together, be – what's the cliché – one big happy family?

FLORRIE. Yes, miss.

MINA. Call me Mina! Florrie, we want but one year to a brand new century, times are changing, we'll have no more mistress and servants, I don't believe in them.

FLORRIE. No, miss. (*Pause*.) You will still pay my wages?

MINA. Course we will, silly goose… Florrie, Florrie, I know my sister is… a little odd sometimes. Will you help me?

FLORRIE. With Miss Lucy?

MINA. With Lucy.

FLORRIE. Yes, mi – (*Uncomfortably.*) Yes, Mina.

MINA. She has a shadow. (*Pause*.) On her lung… Such night sweats. You must have noticed how thin and frail she is and last winter she coughed up blood. Papa bought Heartwood soon as Doctor Payne made his diagnosis. Poor Papa, he did not realise how ill he was himself. Lucy always was a daddy's girl. And he'd have done anything to make her well. The sea air and so forth.

FLORRIE. Well, he was right to buy Heartwood. Whitby's air is a right famous curative – one the toffs'd bottle and patent and make a bob or two, if they could. A tonic, them sea breezes. Clear the cobwebs.

MINA. Doctor Seward, her fiancé, says we have to be very, very careful. We must keep our dear Lucy away from the chills of the evening or the dampnesses of dawn.

Enter LUCY *in floods of tears*.

FLORRIE. Why, Miss Lucy, whatever is the matter?

MINA. Lucy!

LUCY. Oh why oh why can't they let a girl marry three men at once, or at least as many as want her?

MINA. Three!

LUCY. Poor Edgar Holmwood asked me to marry him yesterday. He was so sweet, Mina, I broke his heart. And when he saw me cry he said he was a brute for upsetting me. And today Quincey Morris! (*Sobbing*.) Oh, Quincey, I am so sorry, but I am promised to Doctor Seward whom I love more than all the world.

FLORRIE. I should've thought you'd enjoy being so proposed to, Miss Lucy.

LUCY. Oh, Florrie, I am so miserable.

FLORRIE. There, there.

MINA. Oh, Lucy, don't be so silly! Don't be so shallow.

LUCY. Shallow!

MINA. Lucy, I'm sorry, I'm very tense, I'm... not quite myself... I'm... going for a walk, I'm... going past the post office. I'll stop to see if there's any mail. Florrie! Florrie, look at the mess in there. Things everywhere! Go tidy it up!

FLORRIE (*beginning to go, slightly sarcastically*). Yes, Mina.

MINA (*exiting, calling as she does*). Change the flowers in the drawing room! Straighten those antimacassars in the parlour!

FLORRIE. Yes, miss!

LUCY. You mustn't mind Mina, Florrie.

FLORRIE. No, miss.

LUCY. I know that sometimes she's a little... odd.

FLORRIE. Yes, miss.

LUCY. Abrupt almost. I know she's sharp sometimes, but... she is upset. Naturally. All this time and not a scrape of the pen from Jonathan. But she means well, Florrie. We're both terribly pleased with you.

FLORRIE. Yes, miss.

LUCY. I didn't think we'd find anyone else who'd do for us.

FLORRIE. Oh, there's always someone who'll do. Your fine suitors'll find that out, Miss Lucy, never fear. You might even find yourself insulted how quick they forget you.

LUCY. I don't think so, Florrie!

FLORRIE. No, miss.

LUCY. *Do* change the drawing-room flowers. Those lilies are so funereal! Something pretty to cheer Mina up.

She exits.

FLORRIE (*picking up behind them*). Don't believe in servants? Oh, don't believe in servants, don't you, that's very interesting. Better pinch yourself, Florrie my girl, look in the mirror, pinch yourself to see if you're real.

Scene Nine

DRACULA*'s castle.* JONATHAN *is shaving. He has taken up a wooden-backed mirror with handle from his luggage and has lathered up his face. Now he shaves with an open razor. He moves the mirror around (he is facing us, we see the back of the mirror) so that he would certainly see in the mirror anyone behind him.* DRACULA *approaches him, silently, but certainly in his mirror's field of vision.* DRACULA *is right at* JONATHAN*'s shoulder.* JONATHAN *looks round, sees him, looks back in the mirror, doesn't see him, registers horror, drops the mirror. It smashes.*

DRACULA. Ah, seven years of good luck! I trust you're getting enough sleep? You are comfortable in Castle Dracula? You sleep well and you dream well? But you have cut yourself, so careless, when shaving. This little ruby trickle, it trickles down your throat and –

He reaches out, glittering and fascinated, for JONATHAN*'s throat, and catches the beads of the crucifix. It swings out of the open neck of his shirt.* DRACULA *recoils.*

You have not thrown away this cheap toy yet? Jonathan is very sentimental. Be careful how you cut yourself. It is more dangerous than you think in this country. You will remember.

JONATHAN. Count Dracula, you have to let me go.

DRACULA. Jonathan… but you know I love to have you here. Stay till morning.

JONATHAN. Why may I not go tonight?

DRACULA. Because my coachman and horses are away.

JONATHAN. Count Dracula, please…

DRACULA. But certainly, Jonathan, if you are uncomfortable here you must leave at once.

JONATHAN. You'll let me go?

DRACULA. Of course. Open the door immediately, here is my key.

He gives him the key, makes JONATHAN *open the door for himself.* DRACULA *snaps his fingers and whistles softly as a man does to a dog. The howling of wolves.*

Goodbye, goodbye, my dear friend. As they say, 'Welcome the coming, speed the parting guest.' What? You do not go? Let's sleep on it, eh? (*A sweet smile.*) But let me advise you, sweet Jonathan. Do not try the locked doors. This castle is old, it have many memories. Sleep only in your own chamber. Because here, as elsewhere, there are bad dreams for those who sleep unwisely.

He exits through the door with the howling wolves crescendoing in the swirling fog, whistling and clicking his tongue at them like a shepherd to some faithful collies. JONATHAN *slams and bolts the door and sinks to his knees with his ironic taunting key in his hand.*

JONATHAN. Oh, Mina, Mina, Mina...

Strange music of the vampire-brides theme and the VAMPIRE BRIDES *appearing unexpectedly somewhere. In tattered and browning and even slightly bloodstained lacy bridal dresses, their hair all fluffed out and them painted up red-lipped, white-faced and hectic. They are quite recognisably horrid versions, perversions, of 1.* MRS MANNERS, 2. FLORRIE *and 3.* LUCY, *led by her. In fact, they are everyone from the Whitby family but Mina. They whisper together and laugh with a silvery, unreal, glassy, electronic laugh: 'like the intolerable tingling sweetness of water-glasses when played on by a cunning hand' writes Bram Stoker.*

VAMPIRE BRIDE 2. Go on, you are first, and we shall follow. Yours is the right to begin.

VAMPIRE BRIDE 1. He is young and strong. You first.

VAMPIRE BRIDE 3. You think so? Shall I leave you some?

VAMPIRE BRIDE 2. There are kisses for us all.

VAMPIRE BRIDE 1. Plenty.

VAMPIRE BRIDE 2. A sweet sufficiency.

VAMPIRE BRIDE 3. Give it to me, Jonathan.

JONATHAN. Who – are – you?

He gives her the key. She kisses it and puts it in her bosom, leans over him.

VAMPIRE BRIDES. Who! Who! Who!

They laugh.

Who…

It is a whisper of erotic horror. He moans.

JONATHAN. Lucy?

JONATHAN *is lying back in thrall.* VAMPIRE BRIDE 3 (LUCY) *advances and bends over him – now, this is more straight out of Bram Stoker and can't be beat for atmosphere or stage direction – 'until he can feel the movement of her breath upon him… sweet, honey-sweet, sending the same tingling through the nerves as her voice, but with a bitter underlying the sweet, a bitter offensiveness as one smells in blood'.* JONATHAN *is 'afraid to raise his eyelids but looks out and sees perfectly under the lashes'. While* VAMPIRE BRIDE 3 *'goes on her knees and bends over him, fairly gloating. There is a deliberate voluptuousness which is both thrilling and repulsive, and as she arches her neck she actually licks her lips like an animal till he can see in the moonlight the moisture shining on the scarlet lips and on the red tongue as it laps the white sharp teeth. Lower and lower goes the head as the lips go below the range of his mouth and chin and seem about to fasten on his throat. Then she pauses and her tongue flickers in and out and her hot breath is on his neck.* JONATHAN*'s flesh tingles and he feels the soft shivering touch of lips and the hard dents of two sharp teeth just touching and pausing. He closes his eyes in a languorous ecstasy and waits with a beating heart.' Quote, unquote.*

Enter DRACULA. *He grasps the neck of* VAMPIRE BRIDE 3, *cuffs the others back. They are breathing, almost snarling.*

DRACULA. How dare you touch him, any of you? How dare you cast eyes on him when I had forbidden it? Back, back all of you. Back. Give. Back.

She hates to, but gives him back the key.

VAMPIRE BRIDE 3 (*with a 'laugh of ribald coquetry'*). You yourself never loved. You never love. You cannot love.

All three VAMPIRE BRIDES *join in 'a laugh of such mirthless hard soul-lessness that it almost makes* JONATHAN *faint to hear. It sounds like the pleasure of fiends.'* (*More quotes straight from Stoker…*)

DRACULA. Yes, yes, I too can love. You yourselves, you can tell it from the past. Is it not so? When I am done with him, you shall kiss him at your will. Now go.

VAMPIRE BRIDE 3. And us? Are we to have nothing tonight?

With a low laugh she points to the bag on the floor which he has tossed down. And in which something moves, hideously. DRACULA *nods assent. She lifts it up, opens the neck of the bag. Crying of a baby. All three laugh and crowd round it and scurry off, quarrelling over it skittishly, still laughing.* JONATHAN *slumps.* DRACULA *picks up the fainted* JONATHAN *in his arms as in a pietà.*

Scene Ten

A composite scene, simultaneously, Heartwood House, Stoneyfields (Bedlam) and the Castle. In Bedlam now, though, RENFIELD'*s song will stitch together all the mostly wordless strands of* JONATHAN *deciding to flee and disappearing from our ken and the static anguish of* MINA'*s wait.*

RENFIELD *is singing 'Loving Mad Tom' in the moonlight. In his cell. Very sweetly.*

RENFIELD (*singing*).
>From the hag and the hungry goblin
>That into rags would rend ye.
>The spirits that stand by the naked man
>In the Book of Moons defend ye.
>That of your five sound senses
>You will never be forsaken.

MINA *in Heartwood, in a hell of anxiety, enters.*

JONATHAN (*waking into* his *hell*). Those… women… My God. Help me, I… Mina! Mina has nothing in common with them.

MINA, *in her underwear and barefoot and in her indolence and impotence, wanders round Heartwood.*

RENFIELD (*singing*).
Nor wander from yourselves, with Tom
Abroad to beg your bacon.

JONATHAN. I had the key in my hand and I traded it for a hint of a kiss from that…

He sobs.

MINA. Where oh where are you, my darling…

RENFIELD (*singing*).
While I do sing, 'Any food, any feeding
Feeding, drink or clothing?
Come dame or maid, be not afraid:
Poor Tom will injure nothing.'

MINA. Please be safe…

JONATHAN. The devil and the devil's brides.

MINA. Please, please, please…

A MAID *and* FLORRIE *carry on* MINA*'s half-finished wedding dress as, simultaneously, two* NURSES *and* DRINKWATER *carry bindings and straitjacket to* RENFIELD.

No, Florrie, don't make me.

RENFIELD. Bastard. Bastards try tie a man up, he only sing a sweet song out loud, clear and pure in their fat faces.

But MINA *gets tape-measured and poked and pinned and, sure enough,* RENFIELD *gets straitjacketed.*

JONATHAN. I will get free or die trying!

Terrified, he goes out of the window, disappears.

RENFIELD, *chained and straitjacketed, sings.*

RENFIELD (*singing*).
> With a host of furious fancies
> Whereof I am commander
> With my burning spear on a horse of air
> Through the wilderness I wander…

MINA. It's still so foggy.

FLORRIE. I honestly do think another layer of the Brussels lace, miss, just peepin' out from under… A brool, that's what we call such a fog. A real pea-souper. Spoilin' for a storm, I suppose. Can't see where sea ends and sky begin…

MINA. Can't see a blind thing. Nothing.

FLORRIE. All grey, except the grass standin' out that hectic green and all creation bristlin'. Them foul rags of cloud just hangin' down, that do always be a sign. (*Pause.*) But I do think just the hint of another flounce'll do it, without we get too fancy.

RENFIELD (*singing*).
> In the lordy lofts of Bedlam
> On stubble sweet and dainty…

FLORRIE. Miss Mina, you'll get five letters all at once, you wait and see. It'll be the fog, delayin' the shipping.

> LUCY *enters.*

LUCY. Done my darts yet, Florrie? Fine bridesmaid I'll be.

> LUCY *sees* MINA's *acute anxiety.*

Mina, you're not worrying again? Mr Hawkins said not to. *He's* not. I'm sure Jonathan is fine. And look at your lovely dress! I do envy you.

MINA. It's a dress.

LUCY. Your wedding dress. It's beautiful.

MINA. Oh, Lucy, I don't think I'll ever wear it.

> *She sobs,* LUCY *and* FLORRIE *try and hush her. It begins to get really dark as the girls go off, comforting* MINA, *very much afraid she might be right.*

RENFIELD (*singing*).
> Brave bracelets strong,
> Sweet whips ding-dong
> And wholesome hunger plenty,
> But the moon's my constant mistress
> And the lovely owl my… (*Speaks*.) master.

Silence.

Master?

Silence.

Master master master master master master. Faster. Faster. Faster. Faster. Faster. Faster. Faster-master. Faster-master. Master-faster. Faster. Fasterfasterfasterfasterfasterfaster faster-fasterfasterfasterfasterfaster.

(*Breathes*.) He is coming.

But at Heartwood, in the storm that RENFIELD, *on behalf of* DRACULA, *has been brewing up, re-enter a now night-shirted* LUCY, *sleepwalking,* MINA *after her.*

MINA (*whispering*). Lucy, Lucy, back to bed, my love, it's not morning yet…

LUCY. Coming, coming, coming, coming, coming.

MINA. Come, Lucy. Come on.

A sudden streak of lightning and the wind bashes the window open with a frightening crash. LUCY *shrieks, waking up.* MINA *hugs her.*

LUCY. What happened, Mina? What's happening?

MINA. You've been sleepwalking again, sweetheart. Nothing to be frightened of. Come back to bed. Mina's here. Ssh! It's only thunder rumbling, it's all right.

Storm starts in earnest. LUCY *and* MINA *looking out, terrified. Thunder, lightning, wind. And louder.*

LUCY. Mina! Oh, Mina, look!

RENFIELD. Fasterfasterfasterfasterfaster. Master!

Huge bang (of ship slamming ashore). Whiteout then black.

Scene Eleven

Lights up on blasted-clean morning. Beautiful light. FLORRIE *and* MINA, FLORRIE *helping* MINA *dress.*

FLORRIE. Last night though! Such a storm! What stories people do tell! Down at the dairy this mornin' everybody was all agog about that ship. Nonsense and superstition. Nobbut one dead man lashed to the wheel! Hands stiff round a crucifix, its chain wound so tight said it were cut clean through to white wristbone. And in his pocket, writin'. Writin' 'bout how ship was haunted. One by one sailors jess... overboard or eaten. Must've gone mad on long voyage with lack of vitals! But oh... oh, what a storm, eh? Mother and father of a tempest.

Enter a strange, calm LUCY.

LUCY. And the air this morning is so sweet you'd think it'd never get dark again.

MINA. But that black dog...

FLORRIE. What black dog, Miss Mina?

LUCY. I saw it! As the boat struck the shore it leapt. From down under the hold to dry land in a single bound and off over the north cliffs like black wind.

FLORRIE. Miss Lucy, you all right? You does look pale.

LUCY. Oh, nothing! I've got a visitor... Must have come in the night... My friend, my bloody friend.

MINA. The curse.

FLORRIE. Oh, Miss Lucy, you've come on. Why didn't you say so? Do you feel poorly, poor thing? Cruel, that's what some of them cramps and drags do be. Do you want to lie down, I bring you herb tea and a hot-water bottle?

MINA. Nonsense, Florrie!

LUCY. We've got to learn not to give in to such weaknesses! Exercise! Exercise like the lady doctor in the *Lady's Home Companion* recommends. Swedish callisthenics! And no whingeing or the gentlemen'll never treat us as equals.

MINA. No gentleman need ever know.

LUCY. Don't you always feel… unclean? Friend. Friend. How queer, some friend!

FLORRIE. Indeed, Lucy, and it's many women are pleased to see such a friend. Poor Fanny Waller in our village as was born not right, with a humpback and a harelip and a port-wine birthmark and a good sight more than six and three ha'p'orth short in the shilling so's you'd not have thought a man alive'd been inclined to take advantage of her – she went three months and never had to delve in the rag bag. Till finally her mother made her go to the wise woman to see if she had a growth or an ulcer. Wise woman pressed on her belly – 'And can you feel anything?' says wise woman. 'No, mum, not really,' says poor Fanny, 'just sometimes, oh, somethin' like li'l bird, flutterin'.' 'Well,' says the wise woman, she says, 'And did you not feel that li'l bird go in?' 'No, mum.' 'Oh well, then, by Christ, and ye'll feel it cam back out again!'

LUCY *goes into hysterics of laughter.* FLORRIE *joins in.* MINA *looks disapprovingly but eventually she cracks and all three laugh, wiping tears away, hugging each other.*

FLORRIE. Well, us Eve's daughters got to laugh, I reckon, else we'd sit down and cry.

Enter MRS MANNERS, *the messenger, with a letter.*

MRS MANNERS. Miss Mina. This is for you.

MINA *tears it open. Reads. Held breath all round.* MINA *begins laughing and crying at once.*

MINA. He's safe! He's safe! Budapest. I must go to him. Florrie, pack for me straightaway. One change of dress – I must get tickets.

FLORRIE (*desperately*). Miss Mina, you can't go all way to –

MINA. Budapest. Yes. He's been ill. He's in a convent hospital. But he is better…

LUCY. Where is Budapest? You can't go off to foreign places all on your own. Florrie's right. I'll come with you.

MINA. No! Of course I must! To Jonathan. To – my husband.

FLORRIE. Oh, Miss Mina, are you sure –

MINA. Of course! Oh, Lucy, Florrie, Lucy, Lucy. Laugh for me. My darling is safe.

LUCY. I knew it! I knew it! Oh, Mina, I knew everything would be all right.

Scene Twelve

Bedlam. RENFIELD, SEWARD, NISBETT.

SEWARD. Chloral, nurse. $C^2HC1^3oH^20$. A triple dose. Thrice daily.

NISBETT. Yes, Doctor Seward, sir.

RENFIELD. Doctor Seward, don't go to her. Don't go. Don't leave me. You leave me, I let him in.

SEWARD. Not be long gone, Mr Renfield. It's not as if you're my only charge and concern, you must remember.

RENFIELD. Don't go to her.

SEWARD (*to* NISBETT). Thrice daily for three days, twice daily for two and then twice a week till the mania is abated. Family duties, Mr Renfield, my future bride. You patients forget even we doctors have private lives, eh?

Exit SEWARD.

RENFIELD. She'll let him in and that'll get you! Don't go.

Exit NISBETT.

She sewer-whore, her. Seward, you hear? Oh, sweet Lucy in the daylight, so polite, she got it all sewn up, oh no, no sweat. Come night? They're all mad up in Yorkshire, you know, set of screw-looses, screw-looses – screw Lucy's, who doesn't? She ride them all ragged round and round and round and round and round, East Riding, West Riding, north and south. Forgot to watch her mouth. Swallow his pride. Virgin bride. She'll let him in. That'll get you!

Scene Thirteen

Heartwood House. Sunset going into twilight. SEWARD *carries in* LUCY, *who is indeed not looking very well at all.* FLORRIE *carries bedding, which she settles on the bed with help from another* MAID.

LUCY. Can walk, Arthur, you let me take my time and give me an arm to lean on.

SEWARD. Nonsense, you're light as a feather…

LUCY. Feather floated onto my lap as I sat on the terrace watching all the swallows gather under the eaves…

FLORRIE. Off to Africa.

LUCY. What?

FLORRIE. Winter in the warm…

SEWARD. Once your sister comes back, maybe we'll send you and Florrie off to some spa. Fine ladies, eh?

Now we'll let Florrie make us comfortable, shall we?

He kisses LUCY *a peck on the cheek and, since by now he's settled her in bed, he goes.*

FLORRIE *comes with a mirror.* LUCY *pushes it away.*

LUCY. Florrie, don't! I can't bear to look at myself.

FLORRIE. Once we get the roses back in your cheeks…

LUCY. Don't light that lamp!

FLORRIE. Why ever not, miss? Can't hardly see beyond my own nose.

LUCY. 'Cause all the pretty furred and flying things, they fly into the flame and singe their wings…

FLORRIE. Dizzy articles.

LUCY. Oh, Florrie, I am so frightened.

FLORRIE. Don't say that, Miss Lucy.

LUCY. It was so strange, Florrie!

FLORRIE. Dreaming! Sleepwalking. Could've caught your death out so far at night in nobbut your nightdress.

LUCY. No. No, I didn't quite dream. It felt real. It was real. Through streets, over bridges. A fish leaped as I went by and I leaned over to look at it – and… dogs howling, the whole town full of dogs howling all at once as faster faster faster up the hundred steep steps to the graveyard, the only spot in all the world I felt I ought to be… I was asleep, I… something long and dark with red eyes, like the sunset and something very sweet and very bitter all round me at once and… sinking. Sinking into deep green water, singing in my ears, drowning. Then… everything passing away from me, my soul from my body and it seemed to float about the air. The West Lighthouse was right under me and a, a sort of agonising feeling as if I were in an earthquake and I… I came back and… you, shaking my body. I saw you, saw you do it before I felt it. Florrie!

FLORRIE. Bad dreams.

LUCY. Every night, Florrie, scratching, flapping at the window.

FLORRIE. Moths at the pane, a loose sash rattling, a rat got ahind the wainscot. Miss Lucy, bogies is all kinds of things.

LUCY. Don't tell me it doesn't exist!

FLORRIE. No, no, Lucy, I didn't say bogies didn't exist, I just say bogies is all kinds and sorts of things except bogies.

LUCY. I'm frightened, Florrie.

FLORRIE. No use being frightened.

LUCY. And I think you're frightened too. No, you're sad. Florrie, why are you so sad? Do you miss your sweetheart?

FLORRIE. How do you know I've got a sweetheart?

LUCY. I know things, Florrie. I know more than people think. I'm not just a little girl, Florrie.

FLORRIE. No, miss.

LUCY. Is he a gentleman?

FLORRIE. Who, miss?

LUCY. Your gentleman. Your… lover…

FLORRIE. No, miss, he's a soldier.

LUCY. What's his name?

FLORRIE. Jem, miss.

LUCY. Jem, your precious.

FLORRIE. Suppose he's all right. Sometimes.

LUCY. Florrie? Florrie, do you... let Jem love you?

FLORRIE. How do you mean, Miss Lucy?

LUCY. Oh, Florrie, you know what I mean. I'm not a child. Is it... nice, Florrie?

FLORRIE. Well, suppose it must be, else it wouldn't be so popular.

LUCY. Is it absolutely the most sweetest delicious swoony magical marvellous thing you ever – ?

FLORRIE. It's nice at the time, for sure, Miss Lucy.

LUCY. Oh, Florrie, what's it like?

FLORRIE. Very strange. Very ordinary.

LUCY. Florrie? Florrie, don't you think Arthur is absolutely *the* only man in the world for me? He's so clever, Florrie, a brilliant man, he has *the* most remarkable mind. And he dragged himself up by his own bootstraps, just like Papa! And he's so good. And fair, and so reliable.

FLORRIE. Miss Lucy, I don't think you should talk so, you will tire yourself out a-talking!

LUCY. He steadies me so. Is your Jem steady?

FLORRIE. No, miss.

LUCY. When he goes will you miss him terribly?

FLORRIE. Suppose I will, miss. But he's not gone yet. I'll start missing him tomorrow.

LUCY. But... there's all night tonight, isn't there?

FLORRIE. There's all night tonight. (*Pause. Tentatively.*) Miss Lucy...?

LUCY. Oh, Florrie, of course you can. Our secret! Now I don't expect you… Don't dare come back till after breakfast tomorrow.

A knock at the door, a tentative tap. SEWARD *puts his head into the room. He has a great bunch of roses.*

SEWARD. All decent? Can I come in?

LUCY. Arthur, of course you can. Mmmm. The last roses of summer! Arrange them for me, Florrie.

FLORRIE. Yes, miss.

SEWARD. Eh… Florrie?

He goes to her, away from LUCY*'s bed so she can't hear, aside to* FLORRIE *urgently.*

She's still terribly pale.

FLORRIE. Yes, sir.

SEWARD. Don't you think she's better than yesterday?

FLORRIE. She's… I don't think she's any worse, Doctor Seward.

SEWARD. Florrie… Florrie… Thank you for letting me know.

FLORRIE. Then Mrs Manners did right to write? She weren't sure when I asked her to.

SEWARD. You did the right thing, Florrie. (*Pause.*) I've written to my old professor who lives in Amsterdam… I've asked him to come. Urgently.

During all this, LUCY *has been undoing the hair* FLORRIE *made neat, fluffing it out again, dropping the demure shawl and undoing her nightdress voluptuously again. In a knowing voice:*

LUCY. What are you two plotting about?

FLORRIE goes. SEWARD *back to her bedside.*

SEWARD. Just asking her how her patient is doing.

LUCY. Well, if you want to know about my bowel movements I wish you'd ask me.

SEWARD. Lucy!

LUCY. Oh, Arthur, you are funny, darling! Did Florrie make me
pretty? Do you love me even though I'm sick?

SEWARD. More than ever, sweetheart.

Re-enter FLORRIE *with the vase of roses.*

LUCY. Roses, roses, oh, I do love roses. So sad when all the
pretty petals fall... Mina and I used to gather up all the petals
in the garden when we were little, and put them in a jar with
rainwater and try to make perfume. Did you ever do that,
Florrie?

FLORRIE. Should think all little girls did, Miss Lucy.

LUCY. But after we left it a week it always festered. Stink and
fur! So then we'd turn it into poison. We'd put in... oh, a dead
mouse and, and... pee... and poison-pods from off the lupins.
It was even better fun making poison than making perfume.
Don't you think anyone'd rather?

FLORRIE. No, no, Miss Lucy, I think most people'd prefer the
perfume, only... other's easier.

LUCY. Off you go now, Florrie, and I want you back here when
we agreed earlier, and not a one moment later, do you hear me?

Laughter and collusion between the girls. Exit FLORRIE.
SEWARD *looks anxiously at* LUCY, *then smiles.*

Oh, Arthur, do take me back to London with you. I do want to
come and see all your lunatics you told me all the stories
about.

SEWARD. Lucy, you know I can't. Not yet. Besides, it would
upset you, you know it would. It'd terrify you.

LUCY. Maybe I want to be terrified.

SEWARD. Lucy!

LUCY. Well, Arthur, I do hate it when you... protect me all the
time. Well... I love it but I hate it too. Tell me the story of
mad Mr Renfield again. Tell me his story.

SEWARD. Lucy... But you know it already. Why did I ever –

LUCY. Almost scared the pants off me! Tell me again. I thought it was funny! When I was a little girl I made Papa tell me the same stories over and over.

SEWARD. Lucy…

LUCY. Tell me! Tell me how once upon a time you went into a madman's padded cell…

SEWARD. Lucy! Lucy, Mr Renfield is presently in a private ward. For his own well-being.

LUCY. …and you could see by spreading bits of rations he'd attracted vast hordes of flies, great bloated buzzing beasts with… steel and sapphire on their wings! And the good doctor knew he could not deprive his patient of his pretty pets – so! But the next time doctor came it was spiders! Spiders and great columns of spidery figures written in a notebook recording their tiny lives and deaths. The fattest spiders he fed on the fattest flies –

SEWARD. You realise I broke a confidence telling you? The confessions between madman and psychiatrist are as sacred as those between priest and sinner…

LUCY *is not to be stopped, though.*

LUCY. And one week later, tamed sparrows! *Next* time doctor went to visit, patient down on his knees keening and fawning, and he said, 'Doctor Seward, please, please, can I have a little pussy cat?'

LUCY *laughs.* SEWARD *is appalled.*

SEWARD. Lucy, whatever can have possessed me to tell you such a story?

LUCY. Arthur, Arthur, please stay with me tonight. Please.

SEWARD. Lucy. Lucy, of course I'll stay. I'll stay with you all evening.

LUCY. Arthur, I mean it. Sleep with me. Hold me. Love me all night, Arthur, I am so terrified.

SEWARD. You know I cannot do that. You are ill, Lucy, I cannot take advantage… I have a sacred trust. I cannot break it. What kind of man…? Not in the absence of your sister who is your guardian. Lucy, it is not fair of you to ask me.

LUCY. Arthur – don't leave me alone.

She takes off her nightdress, so he can see her bare breasts, shoulders and arms. SEWARD *backs off as she reaches out.*

SEWARD. Florrie will be here. We'll make her up a cot bed at the foot of yours so that even if you move in your sleep she'll hear you.

LUCY (*crying, desperate*). She won't, she won't! Oh please…!

SEWARD. Lucy, Lucy, I'm going away now. I'll send Mrs Manners in with a little brandy and water… and something special to make you sleep easy. Once you're asleep – once you're asleep I'll sneak back in and kiss you.

Exit SEWARD *and it darkens.* LUCY *has sunk back as if asleep – or feigning sleep. She pulls off her gown and her shoulders are once more bare.*

LUCY. Come in. Come to me, my love. Come in.

Noises. Shadows. Naked, LUCY *gets out of bed with the sheet bundled up in front of her and, sleepwalking, goes to* MINA*'s wedding dress where it hangs on its dressmaker's dummy.* DRACULA *is there, moves from behind it, rips the bridal veil off and embraces* LUCY *with it in his arms, picks her up, wraps her in it and sucks at the wound on her neck. The classic swoon. Blood pumps out of her in a flood, staining that bridal lace, the dropped sheet, soaking them in scarlet. Red petals fall.*

Black.

End of Act One.

ACT TWO

Scene One

VAN HELSING *alone. Packed and ready, with letter, holding it aloft. He crumples it.*

VAN HELSING. Some ordinary Thursday. The smell of new bread. Clean towels. Hot water. Lathering and shaving. My fat pocketwatch with its everyday tick. It say remember, remember, nine-thirty, the university, as regular, the anatomy lesson, I think just time, just time, I take another cup…

And, friend Arthur, your letter. Your letter at my breakfast table leaning against the Dutch Delft, blue and white.

Your letter, franked 'Express' from England, addressed *Van Helsing* in your doctor scrawl.

Your letter which to rip it open makes a tear in this ordinary morning.

Your letter and I taste blood in my coffee.

The lady fades. Seward the doctor does every proper test – leukaemia, lupus, TB, jaundice, anaemia – for every rational disease. All negative. The lady fades. Seward the lover despairs. Arthur, dear friend, I come.

And, old enemy, I come.

I pack the ghastly paraphernalia of my beneficial trade, instruments, stethoscope…

The whole bag of tricks.

And garlic, asafoetida, quantities of consecrated wafer and my crucifix.

Scene Two

LUCY *and* FLORRIE. *At death's door,* LUCY *is, perversely and against-every-last-odds, still beautiful. A huge-eyed beautiful victim. Her hair has been shorn or shaved, as they did for fevers.* FLORRIE *is both exhausted and bereft.*

LUCY. My lovely hair. Daddy always loved it long.

FLORRIE. For health's sake, Miss Lucy. Honest, your Arthur thought he had to do it, he had to.

LUCY. Bleed the cold and shave a fever...

FLORRIE. What an odd girl you are, Miss Lucy.

LUCY. Said he loved it long and loose and me looking like a little schoolgirl.

FLORRIE. Who did?

LUCY. Daddy... Arthur!... Someone...? I forget... (*Pause.*) Dead and coiled in a box.

FLORRIE. Who?

LUCY. Loved me like a schoolgirl... Wonder if he'll love me like a little boy... My big fat chopped-off braid in a cigar box, glossy as... Quincey Morris's chestnut gelding. That was a man I nearly married. Florrie, did I ever tell you?

FLORRIE. Miss Lucy –

LUCY. He was an American... Yankee Doodle, Mina and I used to tease him so, he was so serious! (*Pause.*) Magnificent animal... I used to give him sugar with my hand out flat. I wanted to but I was afraid to ride. (*Pause. Blurt.*) Florrie, go get it, don't want that he should have it, cut off bits of me, it's my hair, mine. Mine. Fetch it! Arthur's desktop... I want to fling it in the fire and see it shrivel.

FLORRIE. Lucy, he said I was to be sure you slept!

LUCY. Mina! Mina, Florrie, Florrie. I want Mina.

FLORRIE. Can't have her. No one knows where she is. You know that.

LUCY. Read it to me again, Florrie… Mina's letter.

FLORRIE. Can't read, miss.

LUCY. Forgot. Forgot, Florrie. Someone read it to me…? Who'll read me…? Want Mina!

FLORRIE. Doctor Arthur read you it over and over and over. You ought to know it off by heart. I do, heard it so often.

LUCY. Forget… tell me it, Florrie.

FLORRIE *snatches it up, holds it out and, not looking at it, bitterly monotones.*

FLORRIE. 'Dear Lucy, I am so happy I am holding my darling husband's hand and we are going to run away for a whole month and hide in some secret cottage. On a mountain. In Switzerland and I will make my poor skinny darling fat on milk and cheese and chocolate and we will talk to no one but the goats and it will be all the honeymoons I ever wanted.'

LUCY. 'Please you and Arthur be as happy as Jonathan and I. All my love, your Mina.'…Mina. Dearest Mina. Florrie, do you think we will be?

FLORRIE. What?

LUCY. Happy.

FLORRIE. I hope so, miss.

LUCY. Where's Arthur?

FLORRIE. He told you, miss. Doctor Arthur's gone to the station to collect his friend from Holland, the professor.

LUCY. Oh yes, I forgot… Florrie, Florrie, I want to go out for a walk. On the cliffs. With the dog. Sea breezes. Wrap me up I want to walk in the graveyard.

FLORRIE. Miss Lucy we be'n't at Whitby any more. You remember?

LUCY. Not Whitby? But the nice dog… a walk…?

FLORRIE. London. London, Miss Lucy. You remember we wrapped you up in shawls and blankets and the train rocked you all night long and Doctor Seward brought you here, where he can get the specialists to come and cure you.

LUCY. Oh yes... Are we in the madhouse?

FLORRIE. Asylum. Stoneyfields Asylum for the sick.

LUCY. The madhouse.

FLORRIE. All the world's a madhouse.

FLORRIE *goes from* LUCY*'s bedside.*

LUCY. Florrie! Florrie, what's the matter? You should be happy. Mina is married and Arthur has gone to meet the man to make me well.

FLORRIE (*waving telegram*). Can't read. Can't read. Don't need to read. Telegram from the military, it mean just one thing. Dead. Dead, you bastard. Torn up bits of you all over some patch of dirt other side of world. Bloody generals! Bloody Empire! Dead and me three weeks late.

Scene Three

Bedlam. GRICE *and* DRINKWATER *and* RENFIELD, *who's almost catatonic.*

GRICE. Crack of dawn again, another bloody fit. Course, you're nice and quiet now, eh, Renfield, ent you? I've told Seward. I told him. Dawn, I said, and sunset, foaming and jerkin', dawn and sunset, regular as clockwork. Nothing. Well save your breath as talk to Seward. No telling him nothin'. Never was. Does he ever listen? Course, he's worried. Worried about the little girlfriend, no wonder... But I can't see as he's got any call to go neglectin' his duties. Doesn't get paid to bother about the girlie, gets paid plenty not to bovver his arse about everybody in here, us included.

They smoke.

Nisbett said last time she were on night duty he escaped again. His nibs did. Lord of the sodding flies, Mr Sparrer-

Eater Renfield. She went in about half past nine or so, about an hour after his sunset shenanigans, to see if it were all quiet and gives him his bromide and cocoa and all she sees is his feet as out he goes 'ead first out the window, bare-arsed in his nightshirt. Course, he can't go far and sure enough they catch him. Next door in Carfax, outside that queer old overgrown chapel-like buildin', pressed up 'gainst that old iron-studded oak door, cooin' like a dove through the chink and whisperin', 'Master, master, I'm here to do your bidding. Now you are near me do not pass me by.'

Religious ones is the worst. When you've been in this job long as I have, Drinkwater son, you'll know as well as I do. I'd rather have ten Napoleons, three Cleopatras and an Alexander the Great than one Jesus Christ Almighty.

She stubs out fag.

Scene Four

VAN HELSING *is overseeing the fine late-nineteenth-century array of bulbed and zigzagging tubes that are joined to* SEWARD, *standing, arm bared, and* LUCY *prostrate. The colour and the life seems to transfer, with the pumping blood in the tubes, which we see fill up from* SEWARD's *side and over to* LUCY.

VAN HELSING. I promise you, Arthur, that whatever the outcome you will one day be happy that you have done everything you humanly can – almost *more* – for her-you-love.

SEWARD. I'd give the last drop.

VAN HELSING. My dear boy, I do not ask so much as that!

SEWARD. But what is it – ?

VAN HELSING. No organic or functional cause. There I agree with you completely. Much blood loss, yet she is no way anaemic… And yet there is cause. Always cause for everything, my friend. This disease – for Not To Be All Well is a disease – interests me much.

SEWARD. And these recurring dreams and her deliria… Bats, black, scratching, sunset – if it weren't that I know that my Lucy's basic mental constitution is every bit as sound as my own, then –

SEWARD *begins to swoon and gasp, faint with his blood loss.*

VAN HELSING. Enough, dear boy, don't try to talk. This spending of your vital energies is enough for now.

LUCY *moans and stirs.*

Hush, girlie, stay under now, not yet… hush…

VAN HELSING *removes the tube from* SEWARD, *stoppers the end of it, then from* LUCY, *rubbing at her wrist, taking her pulse.*

Arthur, a glass of port and rest yourself a while.

LUCY. Arthur, mmm, Arthur, darling.

She sits up, clawing at the black velvet band around her neck. VAN HELSING *looks quickly under it.*

VAN HELSING (*sharply*). Where come this wound?

LUCY. Arthur, oh, Arthur, what happened? Oh… such lovely dreams, Arthur, I could feel you all around me, so close… I feel… I feel like my old self again. I want to get well for you.

VAN HELSING. Miss Lucy, how long you have this wound?

LUCY. Nothing. Florrie scratched me, with a pin, it's getting better. It was an accident.

SEWARD. Were you hiding something from me? Some sore place, Lucy?

LUCY. No. No… I… Arthur, you know I always like to wear this at my throat, it is a fashion that I like.

SEWARD. Hush, don't try and talk, my love.

LUCY. Arthur, I do want to get well.

VAN HELSING. Excellent. Then you help us make you so.

LUCY. Doctor Van Helsing, Arthur thinks I am just a silly little girl, it's all in my head, I make things up.

VAN HELSING. We should send him back to his mad mans, eh? Miss Lucy, young lady, you and I, we know there are more things in heaven and earth than there are dreamed of in his psychology... But now, miss, I want to give you another present to dangle from that so-pretty black velvet band. Will you wear it for me?

LUCY. Ugh, I don't like crucifixes, they are so... morbid. Doctor Van Helsing, this diamond buckle my Arthur gave his mother on the day he graduated, doctor, and she wore it every day until she died. Isn't it lovely? I'm sure it does do me so much more good.

VAN HELSING. Nevertheless, pretty Lucy, I ask you, as you love Arthur – or as you love your own sweet self, to respect my heirloom!

LUCY. But of course, Doctor Van Helsing, if it means so much to you.

VAN HELSING. Wear it always, eh? And here are some pretty flowers, yes? Sweets for the sweet.

He begins garlanding the bedside with garlic.

LUCY. Pretty.

VAN HELSING. But not for you to play with, huh? I am sorry I get sharp with you, these garlands and wreaths I hang by your window... and round your shoulders... and on your bedhead and counterpane. These, Miss Lucy, are medicine.

LUCY. They stink! Pooh. They are as rank as... common garlic.

VAN HELSING. Much virtue in a common flower. The longer I try to live a true man of science, the more sure I am I must not deny the ancient woman wisdom. Just trust. Do not question. Please. For now. Please.

(*Briskly.*) Now, do not disturb this... floral arrangement? Yes? Tonight, even if the room feel so close you think you stifle, do not, not open either the window or the door.

Now, we medical men are going to what? Go back over old case histories. I mean, Lucy, we talk fondly of our old times. I send Florrie in to you, with beef tea I have her prepare and maybe just a thimbleful of that ruby port that put such heart into your intended.

They go from her bedside. She seems quiet. As they exit –

Come, Arthur, if we can get your lovely girl back to her ripe health then old Van Helsing will kick up his heels and dance at your wedding, believe me, never mind his old bones. (*Pause.*) The blood is the life!

– And they have gone. Back at LUCY*'s bedside, she's breathing deeply. It darkens, there's a rattle at the window, silence again.* FLORRIE *comes.*

FLORRIE. Sleepin'. Sleepin' and her not had supper.

LUCY*'s voice is deep, strange and vampire-seductive.*

LUCY. Florrie, Florrie, thank the devil you've come, help me, Florrie. Florrie, I can't breathe.

FLORRIE. Beef tea. Port wine.

LUCY. Florrie, I want to give you a present. It's… it's valuable, Florrie, if you don't like it you can sell it. Sell it and buy things for the baby when it comes – or even buy a ticket to go over the seven seas to find Jem's grave.

FLORRIE. Why'd I care about a grave? He's dead. (*Pause.*) Jesus, how'd you know? I never told – Who told you about baby? I never told a single soul.

LUCY. Florrie, it's pretty! It's a… crucifix, Florrie. Are you a Catholic?

FLORRIE. No, miss, I'm nothing.

LUCY. Florrie, don't say so! Heavy. It's… too heavy, Florrie, ugly ornate old thing, take it off me, please.

FLORRIE. Miss Lucy, I'm sure it can't do you no good to get so worked up about a bauble. (*Takes it off for her.*) I don't want it, mind!

LUCY. Take it! Worth a bit, even meltdown value. Now, these flowers… phew, don't they reek?

FLORRIE. Say that again.

FLORRIE fastens the cross onto herself.

LUCY. Throw them away, Florrie, in the dustbin, and bring me my lavender water and some sal volatile before I faint. Open windows. Clear the air.

FLORRIE gathers up the garlic flowers.

FLORRIE (*exiting*). You've got to sup every drop, mind, it's full of goodness…

LUCY breathes, asleep, and soon, suddenly, DRACULA comes to her. She makes an exultant sound and reaches out as if in love. He pushes her back on to the bed, takes one last cruel drag at the dregs of life in LUCY. She flutters in struggle, then is still. He drops her, goes.

Scene Five

LUCY's room. Morning. Flooding light. She's lying across the bed. Half out of it. Neck and throat, with its blood traces and wound, bared. Enter FLORRIE with a pitcher and ewer. She sees this, screams.

FLORRIE. Doctor Seward? Doctor Seward, Doctor Van Helsing, come quick!

They enter, minister to LUCY. VAN HELSING sees the crucifix is gone.

VAN HELSING (*to himself almost*). May God forgive! Whoever robbed this maiden, took more than a trinket. Robbed the living and the dead even more than the dying.

FLORRIE holds out the crucifix.

FLORRIE. Well, you may take it back. I never stole it. Florrie Hathersage, as long as she lived, never stole nothing from no one. Miss Lucy gave it to me, wouldn't take no for an answer, I didden want it.

VAN HELSING *takes it back in sorrow, forgives* FLORRIE *with one touch to her face.* LUCY *moans – suddenly alive.*

LUCY. Mina! Want Mina. Big sis… I want Mina. Arthur, why couldn't you bloody save me?

SEWARD *sobs.*

VAN HELSING (*aside to* FLORRIE, *urgently*). The sister and the husband, they have traced them yet?

FLORRIE. No, sir, they've been tryin' every way. Doctor Van Helsing, is Miss Lucy going to die?

VAN HELSING. Very well, we cannot find them. So we can with clear conscience let wax and wane their honeymoon.

LUCY, *in sudden superhuman fit, gets herself out of bed.* VAN HELSING *reels back. He and* SEWARD *run after her as* LUCY, *in her final mania, runs zigzag.*

LUCY (*calling*). Mina! (*Screaming.*) Mina, Mina!

LUCY *falls to the ground.* VAN HELSING *and* SEWARD *pick her up.*

VAN HELSING. Oh, Lucy, Lucy…

SEWARD. For the love of God, Van Helsing, tell me how to save her.

VAN HELSING. She's fading, Arthur, no more blood…

SEWARD. There is a kind of animal strength to her and I can't believe she will ever die.

LUCY *is in the 'stertorous-breathing', almost growling, sleep, with her lips drawn back, her teeth bared. Then, without waking, though her eyes may flicker open and shut again, in a 'voluptuous voice which has never been heard from her lips' – one like that of the vampire brides in the castle –*

LUCY. Arthur! Oh, my love, come to me, come with me. Kiss me!

SEWARD *goes to kiss her but* VAN HELSING *catches him by the neck and hands and drags him back with superhuman strength as a 'spasm of rage flits like a shadow over* LUCY*'s face and her sharp teeth clamp together'.*

VAN HELSING. Not for your life. Not now. Not for your living soul and hers.

LUCY *breathes. Breathing more gently, wakes up – very weak and faint but sweet old* LUCY *– and puts out her hand to* VAN HELSING.

LUCY. My true friend, thank you… my true friend and his. Guard him. Guard him always, save him and give me peace… Arthur, Ar-thur… I… I love you, Arthur, I wanted to get well for you.

VAN HELSING. Thank God. She wake. Kiss her, Arthur, on the forehead, and once only.

He does. Stands back. Their eyes hold. Hers close. LUCY*'s breath, a burst of death-rattle, then ceases.* FLORRIE, *by herself in the corner, sobs.*

SEWARD. It's all over.

SEWARD *and* VAN HELSING *embrace.*

VAN HELSING. She is dead. But it is only the beginning.

Scene Six

JONATHAN *and* MINA *with luggage, blissfully happy, unaware, en route for home and Heartwood.*

JONATHAN. Well, Mrs Harker, do you know what I'm looking forward to?

MINA. No. What does it begin with?

JONATHAN. L.

MINA. I can't think of anything that begins with L.

JONATHAN. Can't you?

MINA. Is it...? Mmm? Loving-Mina-to-bits-on-Mina's-big-fat-goose-feather-bed?

JONATHAN (*laughing*). No.

MINA (*laughing*). No? Cheeky beggar. (*Puts her arms round him.*) I can't think of anything else except love.

They kiss.

JONATHAN. I know. My wife is insatiable. Actually, it is lunch.

MINA. Lunch!

JONATHAN. Mmm. English Sunday lunch. Tomorrow. Roast beef, medium well done, *no* garlic, no herbs, no foreign muck, just a daub of mustard and a couple of cook's best Yorkshire puddings!

He starts to nuzzle into her neck.

MINA. Oh, you are a monster!

JONATHAN. Isn't this the nicest part of going away? Coming back. Isn't it?

MINA. Do you think Lucy will like her little jewelled watch we brought her? Isn't it just Lucy! And the cuckoo clock! Won't Lucy love it? I'm so dying to see my little sis!

Scene Seven

Bedlam. RENFIELD*'s cell.* SEWARD *and* NISBETT *and* REN-FIELD. SEWARD *has a zombie-grim face, a black armband and tie.* NISBETT *has brought case notes and sets them out.*

RENFIELD (*singing*).
  Oh, the rats and the mice and the other small deer
  Their blood it is but very small beer...

SEWARD. How has he been, Nisbett?

NISBETT. Very quiet, sir.

SEWARD. Really? Great… gaps in my notes, Nurse Nisbett, have to get back to filling some of them in.

NISBETT. Nurse Grice and Drinkwater and everybody, sir, we all wanted to tell you how very sorry –

But he bursts in, stopping her.

SEWARD. Thank you, Nisbett. Now, about Renfield.

NISBETT. We hoped you didn't think we was familiar, sending that wreath but she was such a lovely lovely young lady, doctor, and we couldn't help feel really really sad.

SEWARD. Yes. Yes. Well, to work.

NISBETT. I know exactly how you feel.

SEWARD. Yes –

NISBETT. Life doesn't seem worth livin' without someone to love and call your own. Now, I know it looks like nothing but work, work and emptiness – but you're young yet. Well, I'm not suggestin' for a minute you'll ever forget her but –

SEWARD. For Christ's sake, can we just get on?

NISBETT. Time *is* a great healer, though.

SEWARD. Get me Renfield's charts.

NISBETT. I sometimes fancy they can tell us things. Oh, I know it's stupid, really, but sometimes I thinks mad talk is just like… moon talk or baby babble and if we only had the lingo – well, he looks at you sometimes so wise, like an ape in a zoo. I'm sure Renfield ent so green as he's cabbage-lookin'.

SEWARD. Now, go away, will you, please, Nurse Nisbett, and leave me with my patient.

A slightly offended NISBETT *shrugs and exits.*

RENFIELD. Doctor Seward, excuse me, but it's time for me to love you and leave you, time to say toodle-pip, au revoir or should I say adieu-arrivederci-if-you'll-just-arrange-for-the-old-trousers-and-topcoat-to-be-returned-to-me-forthwith-I'll-be-off-good-and-sharpish. He wants me to be an instrument of evil, but I've changed my tune. And him not one to take no for an answer. He is at hand. At hand? At throat, he is at it! Next door, next week, upstairs, downstairs and in my lady's chamber. So, as I don't want to be party to any of that, I'll just be off, okay?

SEWARD. Mr Renfield, you are detained here for your own safety. And the safety of others. You, Mr Renfield, are a paranoid schizophrenic with alternating homicidal and suicidal phases. And zoophagous to boot. How is the old diet, eh? Still crunching up those tasty bluebottles?

RENFIELD. Flies! Get knotted, doctor, I'm not wanting to talk fizzing trivia with you, don't you understand?

SEWARD. And yet once upon a time... once... upon a time, flies were your sole interest.

RENFIELD. Soul? Soul? What do you want to talk about flaming souls for? I don't want anything to do with souls.

SEWARD. Good. Because there is no such thing. I am a doctor and I have never seen a soul. I have been inside every inch of the human body, filleted it and turned it inside out and I have yet to see hide nor hair or even hint or sniff of even the most vestigial or atrophied 'soul'.

RENFIELD. I pray thee, Lord, my soul to take... My soul to take, my soul to make, my soul to shake. (*Pause.*) My heart to break, my soul to wake. (*Pause.*) Doctor! My heart to *break*, my soul to wake! Understand? (*Suddenly lucid.*) Did you know the ancients – realising the aerial powers of the psychic faculties, imagination and, indeed, 'soul' – portrayed it as a winged thing, as *butter* – or even *common* – fly?

SEWARD. Flies! That's what I want to talk about. Forget the soul!

RENFIELD. The whole trouble with modern man, that. Makes him easy meat, believe me. I don't want no fizzin' souls. Life's all I want. Life's all right. I have all the life I need, right now, I'm laughing. (*Starts to sob.*) I don't want nobody's soul on my conscience. Doctor! Nothing in a soul to eat or – No!

SEWARD. Or what? Drink? Drink? Eat... or drink? Why won't you say the word 'drink'?

RENFIELD, *sobbing, covering up his ears.*

Why are you afraid of being burdened with a soul?

A wail from RENFIELD.

Why are you so sure you will have 'life' in the future? Who has promised it to you? Who?

He grabs RENFIELD *by the throat.* NISBETT *enters.*

NISBETT. Doctor Seward, Doctor Seward, I never saw you! I never saw you ill-treat a patient.

SEWARD *desists.* RENFIELD *is a sobbing heap on the floor.* SEWARD, *looking at his hands. The horror.* SEWARD *runs away with a sob, as* MINA *in a black dress, weeping, with* JONATHAN *by her side, enters. Hearing her,* SEWARD *goes grimly towards her, as the lights go down on* RENFIELD*'s cell.* MINA *and* SEWARD *meet and embrace, weeping, as a miserable, grim and set* JONATHAN *stands by them, touching first one then the other's arm, uselessly.*

SEWARD. Oh, Lucy, Lucy. Lucy.

MINA. Lucy.

MINA *weeps, hugged close to him.*

Scene Eight

VAN HELSING *alone. Watching the mourners, unseen, he is crying and then laughing his black ironic 'King Laugh'. As described in Bram Stoker's book, he 'raises his hands over his head in a sort of mute despair, beats his palms together in a helpless way, finally sits down on a chair and, putting his hands before his face, begins to sob with loud, dry sobs that seem to come from the very racking of his heart. Then he raises his arms again as though appealing to the whole universe.'*

VAN HELSING. Poor lily-white Lucy who never did no one harm.

What is it, amongst us, in the darkness, sent down from the pagan world of old that such things must be?

He laughs his laugh again.

King Laugh, I laugh him one last time! He leave me now, I know it. I go far from the realms of laughter – will I ever see his grim and grinning face again? King Laugh, who comes unbidden, making bleeding hearts, and dry bones, and tears that scald as they fall, dance to your tune. King Laugh who make Van Helsing chuckle as the earth thud on Lucy's coffin. King Laugh who shares this knowing with Van Helsing – when the lover and the sister weep, weep and think of the pain of losing Lucy the worst thing they will ever have to bear. The worst.

He sobs and laughs together.

Oh, my dear friend, be happy in your misery for when you dry your eyes it is to face such pain and trials you cannot dream of. And I must enlighten you how deep the darkness. Oh, sister, lover, you should pity me, because *I know*.

Scene Nine

Bedlam. RENFIELD, *whispering very quietly and still.* DRINKWATER *and* GRICE *on a tea break with fags and newspapers.*

RENFIELD. I said send Van Helsing send Van Helsing send Van Helsing… else! I tell you, else the consequences… (*Shakes his head and whispers under his breath, so it's all but inaudible.*) Help us helpushelpus…

GRICE. His nibs isn't much bother these days, is 'e? Not that we can depend on it, just enjoy it while it lasts, eh? Seems he's legged the zoo. Yup, set free all the winged pests of creation into the wide blue yonder. (*Sips tea, smokes.*) Ooh, a lot of nonsense in the paper. As per usual. Bloofer lady. Bloofer lady. What is it? I ask you! How do they make them up? Children. Children missin' all night. Listen to this! 'Paper boy Tommy Deakins, aged seven, was last night the third victim since the mystery attack on twelve-year-old flower-seller Polly O'Donnell of Leicester Square.' Flower-seller, oh, yes! I blame the parents, don't you, Drinkwater? Shockin'. 'All three were found in the morning on Hampstead Heath with strayed wits, small wounds in their necks and a story about wantin' to go play with the bloofer lady.' Oh, yeah, and I s'pose 'Ampstead last night was an 'Eath of Fear? Got to stop buyin' 'em and readin' 'em, that's the only solution.

They drain their tea mugs.

Scene Ten

VAN HELSING, MINA *and* SEWARD *have all been involved in the hypnotism of* JONATHAN, *which we come in on at its climax as* JONATHAN *describes exactly the actions of the three brides, and how he felt. During this, first* MINA *and then* SEWARD *too, get appalled, experience extreme jealously, then… guilt at having failed her.*

JONATHAN. I lie back, I lie… she pulls, I jerk. I lie back. I am asleep. I lie! I… wait. Weight. Ton weight, she… heavy. I lie, she light! Light, cobwebs, she light as a feather. She… Her lips, she licks her lips, like a cat, like a wild, wild animal. One, my head – aah! (*It jerks back like when it happened.*) Two, my legs, no! Prise… prising, yes, oh she, she, the third one yes oh she down down down. I say no, I lie! I want. Yes. I want her. Her breath, sweet, too sweet, thick cloy, blood cloy, blood is thicker than – No. Two dents. Hard dents. Sharp teeth, she is about to fasten…

I pretend to be asleep. Yes. Pretend – I am afraid to look, cannot raise my eyelids. I look out. I look under, I see, I see. Perfect… Lucy. Lucy? Not-Lucy.

She whispering, 'I am six hundred years old, I am thousands of years old, I'm not just a little girl.'

MINA *sobs and* SEWARD *gasps.* JONATHAN, *still in his trance, screams out –*

Mina!

Back to Mina. Must. Free me. (*Breathing.*) The key. His coffin. On him. The key. Yes. Bloated. Bloated filthy leech, him lying sated. My hand. In his pocket. Mina, I have the key, I'll come!

SEWARD *looks on, impotent.* MINA *is a closed column of pain.* VAN HELSING *is intent on the job in hand and ministering to* JONATHAN *in his trance.*

VAN HELSING. You will remember everything, everything you have told us. Alpha beta gamma – waking. One two three four *five*. You are awake. You are with your friends, we thank you for your courage in going back to this dark place.

JONATHAN. It's true. (*Sobbing in anguish.*) God help me, it's all true.

VAN HELSING. Oh yes, it's true. And now, dear friends, we know who our enemy is, and who we must destroy. And where we may destroy him.

JONATHAN (*shuddering*). Carfax!

VAN HELSING *nods.*

SEWARD. I cannot believe in… vampires.

VAN HELSING. He throws no shadow. In the mirror he makes no reflection. He has power over the wolves, the strength of ten men or more… Now we see how the evil is come among us. In a mist which he creates out of himself – or as moonlight rays of elemental dust like those evil brides in Castle Dracula…

JONATHAN *puts his head in his hands and sobs.*

JONATHAN (*crying out*). Oh, Mina, Mina, I went through hell to get back to you.

He reaches out. She moves from him. SEWARD *puts his arms round her. She sobs.*

(*Pleading.*) Arthur, help me!

SEWARD *turns his face away.* JONATHAN *is forsaken, distraught.*

VAN HELSING. My friends, forgive. When you forgive, then we have each other. And our enemy has nothing to match this. With all his hellish powers he is not free. He may not enter anywhere unless first his host shall invite him in. First you have to invite him in. Yet ever after, he in-out as he please!

SEWARD. Oh no.

VAN HELSING. Arthur, he tricked her! No fault, no flaw. A natural thing, the touch of the moon on her skin, the dark kingdom of sleep opening her to things sweet daytime reason says she must resist – at such times mere virtue alone cannot be proof against his powers.

JONATHAN (*in despair*). His almighty power!

VAN HELSING. Not *almighty*. No!

JONATHAN (*with scorn*). Garlic and the crucifix?

VAN HELSING (*confidently affirmative*). For these are the things which so afflict him that his every power shrivels. A stake in the heart, a cut-off head, and that's how we make him true dead. And then and only then can this – as salt does to a snail – dissolve him: the consecrated wafer, the Communion Host. These are the rules. Come dawn he must lie low all day every day in his coffin, shamming death. And remember – wolf, black dog, bat, a fog that choke us – he can only shape change in the darkness. And we can only ever kill him in the light. We do not know why these things are so, but they are so.

JONATHAN. I know it.

VAN HELSING (*offering his hand*). My friend.

JONATHAN. Arthur, I saw with my own eyes. Mina, I made myself forget it but it's true. Arthur, you don't know what it is to doubt everything, even your own sanity, especially your own self.

VAN HELSING. Jonathan, I think it is not time yet we wrestle with Arthur's unbelief. We will prove to him. Perhaps this night, God willing... Madam Mina, I want you should go to bed now and rest.

MINA. No. What is it? My God, what more is there?

VAN HELSING. We must fight together in different ways. We will leave you here protected by every most ancient charm and good so that nothing – no one – can cause you harm unless you yourself overturn it by you ask him in. You understand?

JONATHAN. Where are we going, Van Helsing? Can you promise that Mina will be safe?

VAN HELSING. With such ancient protection there can be no danger. He had to come here because where he lives, everybody knows the charms to guard the door.

MINA. Why is my sister dead?

VAN HELSING. He takes her when she is all unconscious... He sucks secretly at her, stealing from her sources-she-does-not-even-know-that-she-possesses. *But you know*. And if knowing alone does nothing to protect you, then the garlic and the crucifix will.

JONATHAN. Mina, my darling –

MINA. Keep away from me. Go away! Stay with the men.

She exits. The two men are devastated.

VAN HELSING. The good God made this pain for a purpose.

(*Briskly. Brandishing the newspapers.*) You have read these papers? Good! Then... we cloak ourselves, we arm ourselves, and go.

SEWARD. Newspapers? These –

JONATHAN. 'The Bloofer lady'... Yes... of course... of course...

SEWARD. This lurid fantasy of the purple press! All rational men would call it so. I thought we were rational men. These 'small holes, minor wounds in the throats of these tiny victims – such as might be made by a rat or small dog' – these were made by the same as made the hole in my Lucy? You say this?

VAN HELSING. Oh no. It is worse. Far worse.

SEWARD. In God's name, what do you mean?

VAN HELSING. Arthur. These were made *by* your Lucy.

Scene Eleven

Bedlam. RENFIELD, *rocking and rhyming.*

RENFIELD.
> There was a young gel of Nunhead,
> Who awoke in her coffin of lead.
> 'It is cosy enough,'
> He remarked in a huff,
> 'But I wasn't aware I was dead.'

RENFIELD *leaps to his feet and uses his own version of* VAN HELSING's *'King Laugh' to fuel a superhuman leap that breaks his chains and, sobbing and laughing, he escapes.*

Scene Twelve

Elsewhere in Bedlam.

MINA *is trying – and failing – to pray, muttering with clasped hands.*

MINA. Our Father, our Father, our Father, our Father, which art… Oh God! … if I should die before I wake I pray the God my soul to take. Now and… now and at the hour of my death. God help me. God help me I have forgotten how to pray!

Suddenly, from all over, multiple positively Pentecostal voices.

VOICES. Mina! Mina! Mina… Mrs Harker, listen… Let me in, let me in let me in quick Mina Mina Mina quick let me in.

MINA *shrieks.*

MINA. No. Get away from me. You cannot come in, I do not invite you.

Rattling at door, handle-turning. MINA, *bolt upright, making sign of cross. Door opens and in leaps* RENFIELD. MINA *screams a strangled scream that doesn't get out.*

RENFIELD. Quick! You have to get away from here. Sweet lady, I stand here, Renfield, me, your true friend, saner than I ever was in all my life. You must believe me. You are a woman, you have to make them listen. He is come among us. He can kill us all. You have to make them see.

MINA. Tell me what to do to save us all?

She takes his hands. Incredible relief floods through RENFIELD.

RENFIELD. Listen to me. Tell them. Listen to me! (*Pause.*) The blood is the life, that was my motto! I am myself an example of a man who had a strange quasi-belief: a certifiable delusion. To wit, I fancied life to be a positive and perpetual entity indefinitely – even infinitely – prolongable by consumption of multitudes of living things no matter how low in the scale of hierarchical creation –

GRICE *and* DRINKWATER *enter.*

GRICE. Now, now, Mr Renfield, ent polite to disturb nice ladies in their night attire; or their private chambers.

DRINKWATER *has already grabbed and fastened him.* GRICE *sticks a great hypodermic in him. He slumps.* DRINKWATER *drags him off.*

Sorry if he caused you much alarm, Mrs Harker. Actually he's madder than a broom-cupboard of brushes but I doubt if he's harmful in any way. Not to us ladies, if you get my drift. I'll report this, course, in the morning, and someone up in Level Five will get their jotters over this, rest easy about that.

GRICE *goes.* MINA, *in frustration and terror, agitated, alone.*

Scene Thirteen

LUCY's grave, nearly dawn. JONATHAN, SEWARD and VAN HELSING.

SEWARD. See. All this long night and nothing!

VAN HELSING. Keep watch.

JONATHAN. Van Helsing, I shall never forgive myself that it was my transaction granted him his Carfax!

VAN HELSING. Never forgive! I hope you will, my friend. To luxuriate in guilt is an indulgence. You may be sure that these rituals we have this night completed together have sterilised every inch of his home here in the heart of England and rendered it inhospitable to him for ever.

SEWARD. Men of science! Crawling among cobwebs, nailing crude crucifixes on every cupboard door, crumbling Communion wafers in every corner like mothballs in a wardrobe! Were it not so pathetic it would be ludicrous.

JONATHAN. Arthur, I tell you again: I know. I know that it is true.

SEWARD. I don't doubt for a minute the reports are 'true'. We have an epidemic here, all right. The contagion of hysteria. And we are party to it. Grown men!

VAN HELSING. Oh no. Not 'simple girlish hysteria', my friend, believe me.

SEWARD. Imagine a Dark Ages Europe of superstitions and plagues and survivors! Moans from a tomb meant someone had been far too quick to bury their not-yet-dead. Vampires exist. Vampires exist where men believe them to. You ask me if such phenomena occur; I say, beyond question. Ask me if they are supernatural, I say no. I –

JONATHAN. What is it?

SEWARD. No.

VAN HELSING. Yes. Dear Christ.

And LUCY, *lovely and terrifying and ethereal, mist at her toes, comes, almost floating, a rude, ragged and palpable* BOY *and* GIRL CHILD *by each hand. They are sort of sleep-walking. When she sees* VAN HELSING, SEWARD *and* JONATHAN, VAMPIRE LUCY *'draws back with an angry snarl, her eyes blaze with unholy light and her face becomes wreathed with a voluptuous smile'. She drops the hands of the* CHILDREN *and laughs softly, advancing very very slowly.* SEWARD*'s hands cover his face.* JONATHAN *backs off in terror and memory of that time in Castle Dracula with his vampire bride…*

LUCY. Come. Come with me, Arthur. Come to me, my arms are hungry for you. Leave these others and come to me, my husband, come.

SEWARD *drops his hands and opens wide his arms, but* VAN HELSING, *crucifix out and between them, leaps.* LUCY *snarls and recoils into the black and disappears into thin air. The two* CHILDREN *each give one single sob, wake.* VAN HELSING *takes each by the hand.*

VAN HELSING. Ssh, bad dreams, darlings…

He passes them on to JONATHAN.

Arthur. Listen to me, Arthur. That was not your Lucy.

SEWARD. She said to me, 'Come.'

VAN HELSING. Do you understand what I say?

SEWARD. No! I want her.

He sinks to his knees in despair.

VAN HELSING. That is a foul being in her form. Not she! As long as this undead exists, your sweet Lucy's soul shall never have peace. Tell me, am I to proceed with my work?

SEWARD *sobs.*

Tell me. Arthur?

SEWARD. No, please…

JONATHAN. For pity's sake, Van Helsing!

VAN HELSING *takes a* CHILD *to* SEWARD. *Makes him look at him.*

VAN HELSING. Look. This child. And so the evil chain begins to forge itself, Doctor Seward, the contagion spreads! Listen. At dawn we shall make true dead your lover and every little child she sucked at will cure. As yet she caused no death. So Lucy adds not even one fledgeling vampire to the foul horde and I promise you she shall sleep in sweet peace as she deserves. Am I to proceed?

SEWARD. Yes. God help me, yes.

JONATHAN. Where is she?

VAN HELSING. Gone. Far from here tonight. But, come dawn, she be back, asleep, the living dead inside this tomb.

JONATHAN. We will hammer home that stake and kill her truly dead. So she shall never rise again.

VAN HELSING. Tomorrow, in light of day, when we shall return here, Arthur, yours shall be the hand that restores Lucy to us as a holy not an unholy memory. And now, these children, we must see them safe. Only when we have crossed tomorrow's bitter waters do we have any right to hope that some day we shall reach the sweet.

Scene Fourteen

MINA *again. It is still night. She is in terror, still in her night-dress, in agitated wandering. Door rattles and very softly:*

RENFIELD'S VOICE. Mrs Harker, listen! Renfield, Renfield at your door. Mrs Harker, I am your true friend, who has good news for you. I escape! Open the door and let me in.

MINA. Yes. Yes, my friend. Come in!

Through the door bursts DRACULA, *who has an almost naked and tightly gagged* RENFIELD *on a lead like a dog, muffling and gasping.* DRACULA *sweeps in, slams the door.*

DRACULA. Thank you. For your kind inviting. So. You know I
can change my form, but you did not know I can change my
voice too? I can whisper in your ear in the voice of your own
conscience. Renfield be very useful. Good fetch and carrier
for his master. He snuffle out the garlic and foul herbs for me,
throw them away, and turn upside down the crucifix enemy
Van Helsing tack on your door. As if that be enough to keep
me away! I turn everything on its head, sweet lady. Like your
Christ-in-the-Temple I am here to turn tables.

*RENFIELD's hands are manacled. He struggles against his
gags. DRACULA advances on MINA. He takes her in his
arms. She swoons. He sucks at her neck. RENFIELD, in a
paroxysm, bursts his manacles, snaps the chain, tears off the
gag and runs at DRACULA.*

RENFIELD. Laughing with your red mouth! God help me, God
forgive me.

*As he attacks DRACULA, there is a red cloud and RENFIELD
is picked up in the air, whirled around screaming and dashed to
the floor, face down in pool of blood, limbs at all angles. Silence.
MINA comes to. Touches her wet neck. Screams and screams.*

FLORRIE (*offstage*). Mina! Miss Mina. Whatever –

Enter FLORRIE. DRACULA points to RENFIELD.

DRACULA. Mad dog. Bad dog. See what happen when you
won't lie down and lick when master tells you? See what
happens when you savage the hand that feeds you? So it's
Florrie. Looks a bit pale these days. Carrying something. Or
so a little bird told me. White as a sheet, eh? Far as I'm con-
cerned, she's blossoming. Come tomorrow night, my flower,
you'll be ready for the plucking. Lovelier than Lucy and *twice*
as full of life... Madam Mina, though! Husband out and left
her; I've been keeping her a bit of company.

*He takes one small suck at MINA's neck, eyes on FLORRIE,
who's transfixed. DRACULA rips open his shirt as far as his
belly, strokes a gash in himself with his nail and, holding
MINA's hands above her head, forces her to his wound, 'like
a child forcing a kitten's nose into a saucer of milk to compel
it to drink' – Bram Stoker again.*

Out and about. In the night. Pitting their wits against mine. I have them. My herd of cringing jackals scavenging where I have fed. For you, their best beloved one, are now to me flesh of my flesh. Blood of my blood. My bountiful winepress for a while. Soon my companion and my helper for all eternity.

MINA, *choking and gagging.*

Oh, and you will be revenged on them. Not one of them but shall minister to your needs. You will love me for the love they all shall spill for you. Now when my brain says 'come' to you, you shall cross land or sea to do my bidding. You... shall... come.

He closes his eyes. JONATHAN *enters.*

JONATHAN. Mina!

JONATHAN *sinks to his knees.*

MINA. Dracula! God help me.

She grasps at his cloak. Very ambiguous. Almost like an embrace, but also to detain him. Enter VAN HELSING *and* SEWARD *at a burst.* DRACULA *'turns his face and that hellish look leaps into it. His eyes flame red with devilish passion, his nostrils quiver and the white sharp teeth behind the full lips of the blood-dripping mouth champ together like those of a wild beast'. Then 'with a wrench he throws his victim back down' and disappears in as magical a way as can be contrived, leaving his cloak in* MINA's *grasp. She throws it down.*

Jonathan!

JONATHAN *is rooted to the spot, shaking his head.* SEWARD *rushes to her, takes her in his arms.*

SEWARD. Love your living wife.

JONATHAN. You wanted him!

He turns away from her.

VAN HELSING (*over* RENFIELD). Poor brave man, he tried to resist.

FLORRIE *looks down at* RENFIELD *and starts to scream.*

VAN HELSING *holds her by her shoulders. Looks.*

Florrie. Florrie. Tell me. Did he touch you?

FLORRIE. No.

VAN HELSING. Thank God. (*Touches her with sacred wafer.*) Listen, tomorrow we begin to fight him.

FLORRIE. No. (*Backing off.*) No.

She stands rooted. VAN HELSING *touches people with a sacred wafer; first* SEWARD, *then* JONATHAN, *then* MINA. MINA *screams as if branded and, as she turns full-face towards us, distorted in her anguish, we all see, on her fore-head, the mark.*

MINA. I'm cursed.

JONATHAN looks at it with fear and revulsion. VAN HELSING *holds up the crucifix.*

VAN HELSING. We must all be calm and take counsel together.

MINA. I'll kill myself.

VAN HELSING. No, Mina Harker, you must not die. If you die before he is made True Dead, you'll become Undead. Become as he is. One who must blight what he most loves.

MINA *faints.*

SEWARD. In God's name, Van Helsing…

VAN HELSING *kneels, ministers to her.*

VAN HELSING. Madam Mina, forgive me.

MINA *stays unconscious as:*

MINA. Dark. It's all dark. In my box. Lapping water. Little waves.

VAN HELSING. What? 'In my box' – Mina? She is with him! Alpha beta gamma, you will tell us where he is!

SEWARD. Have you no mercy?

VAN HELSING. Hush! This is matter of life and death. More so! Dawn! Mina, where are you? Where?

MINA *speaks in a beautiful seductive voice, right at* JONATHAN.

MINA. Dark. Deep asleep in the dark of my box, sated and snoring off the glut of last night's excesses for we drank deep of each other, sweet Jonathan. Rocked. Rocked on the waters by the little lapping waves.

JONATHAN. No.

MINA *gives a chilling little laugh.*

MINA. Come on, then. Wrap yourself in furs, oh, my enemies, stock up with fat provisions because my wolves are hungry. Van Helsing, better find your sea legs, get ready!

She snores. Stertorous breathing like that of the deathbed LUCY's.

VAN HELSING. One two three – waking. You will remember *nothing*!

He snaps his fingers. MINA *wakes and reaches out for* JONATHAN, *who has backed away from this horror.*

MINA. God help me, what is happening to me?

JONATHAN *cannot look at her. Pause.* VAN HELSING *laughs a burst of 'King Laugh', astounding everyone.*

SEWARD. Van Helsing…?

VAN HELSING (*laughing*). Thank you, my enemy, my friend! You help me. Your blackest cards clean on the table, you deal out such a purity of pain it makes it easy for us all to understand exactly what we have to do. Oh, thank you. Dracula!

SEWARD. Are you mad?

VAN HELSING. Why, I don't know, but you want to help me hunt you down. (*To* SEWARD.) He fears us. He longs for us. He fears us!

SEWARD, *looking at the total splits between each lonely figure; the double chasm between* MINA *and* JONATHAN, *eyes locked and caught: hers pleading, his with hatred as if at betrayal. Mutual anguish.*

SEWARD. He fears… *us*?

VAN HELSING. Oh yes, he fears us! More than we can imagine. Tally-ho, the old fox is wily but we are the hunters who shall pursue him with guile.

MINA. Where is he?

JONATHAN. You know where he is!

MINA *sobs, and breaks from his cruel gaze.* SEWARD *goes to her, puts his arms round her.*

VAN HELSING (*very gently*). You fainted. It was dawn, and you were all unconscious.

MINA. Dawn?

VAN HELSING. You did not know what you said.

JONATHAN. Lying. Lying with him sated and snoring –

VAN HELSING. It was not Mina.

MINA. Where… was I?

SEWARD. On a ship! Van Helsing, it sounded as if –

VAN HELSING. Oh yes! We have put him to flight. Remember he must be *carried* over water, or he cannot cross! We found no trace of his foul catafalque in the cellars of Carfax because already it is cargo and curse to some unsuspecting merchant ship!

SEWARD. But we don't know which ship, which port –

VAN HELSING. But we know where he is going.

Pause.

JONATHAN. Back to his castle.

VAN HELSING. Oh yes! Back to where he is king in his castle and he can wait out the centuries.

SEWARD. We have to go there and stamp him out. Stop the infection at its source.

VAN HELSING. Brave man.

SEWARD. Van Helsing, I am terrified.

VAN HELSING. Good! Then let your true terror give you courage. It is simple now.

SEWARD. Simple?

VAN HELSING. To be brave is to recognise the peril and the necessity. We go. Gentlemen, get ready.

FLORRIE sobs.

MINA. But I am coming too. Blindfold me. Blindfold me to take me on the journey in case… despite myself, without me knowing… I betray all of us to him. But, Van Helsing, if you hypnotise me I can go into him.

JONATHAN. Dear Christ.

MINA. I can tell you where he is.

JONATHAN. No.

VAN HELSING. Oh yes, my friend. All four of us together. Florrie will help us pack and prepare, because it will be a long and a hard journey into the darkest and coldest of the winter-time.

FLORRIE. He'll kill you all. Poor bastard, what kind of a world to be born in.

Though FLORRIE's eyes are on RENFIELD, she is clutching her belly.

VAN HELSING. If first we have to batter down the gates of hell, then we will smash through and kill him so we all, all can live.

He gently turns FLORRIE round and she takes resolve and exits, her arms still hugged round her belly.

But first! Come, Arthur… Daylight is high already.

SEWARD. And I must act in love for my Lucy.

VAN HELSING. Yours shall be the loving hand to give her sweet release.

MINA sobs for Lucy. SEWARD stops in front of MINA, takes her hands. She kisses him as if in blessing. He goes. VAN HELSING takes MINA's hand, pulls her towards

JONATHAN, *turns him, takes his hand, joins theirs solemnly together. But they cannot look at each other for shame.*

Prepare you for the fight.

MINA. Don't touch me, I am cursed!

She would pull away from JONATHAN *and he from her, but* VAN HELSING *has linked them with his strength, and they cannot.* VAN HELSING *touches their hands, which he has joined, then each head in turn, in blessing.*

VAN HELSING. Get ready, for we are *all* going back to that sore place.

Scene Fifteen

SEWARD *performs the ritual of staking* LUCY *in her coffin in the mausoleum. He steels himself. Crosses himself. Does it with deliberation. Just a single stroke. There is a single gasp, a deep sigh or a sort of shudder of* LUCY*'s voice. Certainly nothing violent, not a scream, but a consummation.* SEWARD *sobs with a couple of dry, racking shudders.*

SEWARD. Lucy, my darling, forgive me... I failed you.

Scene Sixteen

NURSES NISBETT *and* GRICE, *during the laying out of* REN-FIELD, *stripping him naked, washing him down, putting cotton-wool in ears and nostrils, keep up a schizophrenic switch back and forward between their two modes, her two modes? Both 'sides' of the single character are, 'good' and 'bad', reconciling themselves into one whole person.* FLORRIE *brings on a basin and works with the* 'NURSES', *one single person, switching from one character to the other.*

GRICE. Dead, eh? Would you credit it? Just on my way off-duty and Seward nabs us. White as this sheet here, he was. 'Nurse! Nurse! There's been a terrible accident.' Some bloody accident!

NISBETT. Sewage pipes. Who'd have thought old Renfield'd commit sewage pipes? I'd've thought 'e'd of been the last, I always says to Drinkwater, such a lust for life he had in him, old Renfield, even at his maddest and most miserable.

GRICE. Must've went beserk and chucked himself down the well of the stair and with one hell of a force to stove his head in and make a mulch of himself like that –

NISBETT. Tragedy, really. (*Pause*.) You get attached. Funny how they've all got their own personalities –

GRICE. In some cases several.

Pause.

NISBETT. Some of 'em, though, when they're gone, so dead you'd think they'd never been alive, others, eh, pinker 'n' realer than ever, 'cept they've not the breath in them to mist the mirror.

GRICE (*to* FLORRIE). Feel sick, girlie? Go on, then, I'll manage. Never seen no one what's croaked before? Get to my age you seen it all –

NISBETT. It's all one to me.

Two women laying out a corpse, FLORRIE *and* NURSE *continue their age-old rituals.*

GRICE. Poor old Renfield! One minute it's professors and doctors queuing up for you wiv pennies-for-your-thoughts, now it's pennies-for-your-eyes, eh?

NISBETT. What you do it now for, though, eh? Me day off. Goin' to a wedding. Would choose the time I'd been invited to a bit of a knees-up. Could've been singin' and 'uggin' and kissin' and rollin' out the barrel 'stead of layin' out a stiff under a windin' sheet.

GRICE. Hey, but we'll miss you, eh, Renfield? Poor mad bugger.

NISBETT. Heigh-ho!

She embraces FLORRIE. *Then she breaks down and sobs.*

Scene Seventeen

Everything is cleared away except DRACULA*'s cloak, black velvet on a bare stage. And, out of the mist and darkness, appear again the heavy gates of* DRACULA*'s castle. Three great thumps at them from behind and they bulge and strain, but hold. Silence after the third battery, and* MINA*'s voice is heard ringing out clearly, from behind these gates at the back of the stage.*

MINA. Stand aside, you men!

The gates fly open wide. The mist clears. MINA, *wrapped in furs and deathly pale, blindfolded, reaching out and moving straight ahead of her. Quite far back, held behind* VAN HELSING*'s outstretched arm, are the amazed-looking* JONATHAN *and* SEWARD. *There are flurries of snow and specks of it on all their clothes.*

SEWARD. She only had to touch!

MINA. We are home now at the black heart of him. I knew it.

JONATHAN *runs to* MINA.

JONATHAN. Mina, my own wife, my brave one.

MINA. Untie my eyes and let me see.

He does so. Even more obvious now is the red mark left by the Communion Host. MINA *holds the blindfold, her eyes still shut. Then opens them, blinking. The others look around, afraid, alert.*

All these weeks in the dark with those I loved, travelling blind. My other senses told me I was on a railway train – the smell of smoke, the sound and vibration of the iron wheels – but behind my eyes I was on the open seas. You fed me oranges; I smelt the peel, spat out the pips, but all the time I tasted blood. Then all around me the noise and bustle of an English port, whilst already in the darkness of my own head I was landed on a European shore. You comforted me in my cabin while all along I sped in a black coach behind a dark driver who whipped six black horses faster than the wind and the wheels hardly bumped on rutted roads. When you crowded me round, protecting me from the gasps and fear and hatred of the inn girls who saw my mark, and you spoon-fed me with stew and rye bread among the babble of foreign tongues, I was already here alone on the high crag of my castle, and when you, my husband, held me tight and tethered to the earth in strange bed after strange bed, while you slept I flew wild and free in the night.

JONATHAN. We will kill him and set you free. And… if we fail, I'll come with you, I won't let you go into the dark alone.

VAN HELSING. Thus this devil can make true married love into something which can swell his ranks. It is very very dark but, thank God, the dawn will soon be here.

DRACULA bursts out of his tomb high up above the gates of the castle.

DRACULA. So, old enemy, you have pursued me till I have caught you. You are standing corn for me to reap.

VAN HELSING and JONATHAN whip out crucifixes, hold them aloft, JONATHAN holding his in front of MINA, who is straining to get free and snarling like a dog, with her eyes flickering horridly, struggling despite herself to go to him. DRACULA coos like a dove.

Pretty one, pretty one… (*Coos.*)

MINA. Yes!

She moans and strains towards him.

SEWARD. Lucy, my love, I'll kill him! Mina!

And SEWARD turns towards DRACULA with a knife, but DRACULA grabs his hand by the wrist and holds it at arm's length, easily.

VAN HELSING. Arthur, wait, the light!

DRACULA. All my darlings, I knew that you would come.

SEWARD. Lucy! I'll kill you in the name of my Lucy.

DRACULA *reaches out the other hand and snaps*
SEWARD*'s neck bone deftly. He falls.* DRACULA *laughs.*
MINA *screams in anguish, and sobs Arthur's name.*

DRACULA. Hush, darling one, later you can feast on his sweet
flesh.

And DRACULA *has waited too long, been too distracted…*
light, rosy light, floods in.

Help me!

He sinks to his knees. VAN HELSING *swiftly grabs the*
equipment and JONATHAN *and* VAN HELSING *rush to*
DRACULA *and despatch him with the stake.* JONATHAN
hammers it home. MINA *is sunk to her knees, sobbing…*

MINA. Oh, my love!

VAN HELSING *goes to her, taking a silver mirror out of his*
bag.

VAN HELSING. Look at yourself!

She stops crying and does so.

The mark! He is true dead. It has gone for ever.

MINA. I am cursed no more!

VAN HELSING *touches her with the Host. She laughs out*
loud in relief.

I'm clean.

VAN HELSING. At last!

VAN HELSING *takes* JONATHAN *and joins them, hand to*
hand, together.

Love each other and live.

They kiss. Then JONATHAN *pulls apart.*

JONATHAN. You wanted him.

MINA. Yes. (*Pause.*) You wanted her.

VAN HELSING. In the name of him who gave his all for you, the best and truest friend any of us will ever know, I tell you to forgive!

He takes them over to SEWARD*'s body and they all look down at it, weeping.*

Sons should bury fathers. You should have taken me!

Sobbing, he crosses SEWARD*'s hands, then goes to* DRACULA. *Looks down.*

God be our witness, when we killed him True Dead it was an act of mercy and not of hate.

JONATHAN. I hate him yet. I hate him. If I could send his soul to burning hell ten times over, then I would and would again.

VAN HELSING. Who wrought all this misery, he is the saddest case of all. Whose victim was he, he made us suffer so? Remember, husband, until today's sweet release she was likely to some day need such pity. Would you have had her denied it by someone with reason for a heart as full of terror and revenge as yours? Forgive! Dracula is dead, long live Mina and Jonathan. May God forgive all his poor creatures, the living and the dead.

JONATHAN *crosses* DRACULA*'s hands just as* VAN HELSING *did his friend* SEWARD*'s. This is something sacred, solemn and final.* MINA *kisses* JONATHAN, *and he her.* VAN HELSING *picks up the hammer and the three stakes, touches the crucifix to his own forehead, then touches it to the hammer and stakes.*

And now his three vile brides.

One final, hellish bit of butchery and God's iciest winds will sear through these ruins and cauterise them clean.

VAN HELSING, *taking the hammer and three stakes, exits through the open gates.* MINA *and* JONATHAN *go to* SEWARD *and look down.* MINA *bends down and kisses his dead face. As she straightens up there is the first screaming screech from the first* VAMPIRE BRIDE *and* MINA *shudders with each echoing blow from the hammer as if it was through her.* JONATHAN *pulls her to her feet, kisses her as a second scream and set of blows ring out. As it stops they fall back and look at each other breathing.* JONATHAN *grasps* DRACULA*'s cloak of darkness and spreads it out at their feet. They sink down on it, kissing. A third and final set of shriek and hammer blows. As it dies away with the lovers entwined on* DRACULA*'s cloak, white snow begins to fall, then blush-pink petals like apple blossom and confetti, then darker purple-pink and finally red, red petals as the curtain falls.*

The End.